50 Quick Tactical Tips for Law Enforcement Officers

Sgt. Clive Milligan (ret)

Copyright © 2023 Clive Milligan

www.bluetrainingsystems.ca

All rights reserved.

ISBN:9798373857017

DEDICATION

This book is dedicated to all those officers who have died in the Line of Duty as well as to their loved ones and colleagues who continue to deal with the profound loss. Their Spirit Lives on in our Training and Work.

TABLE OF CONTENTS

TIP#		page
1 "I'm not going back to jail"		1
2 Visible Handcuff Key		2
3 "You Don't Have any Knives Guns or Hand Grenades on you, do you?"		3
4 Kicking Guns and Knives out of hands after an Officer Involved Shooting		5
5 Too Many Yellers		7
6 Brake Lights Stay On… Beware		8
7 License and Registration Please		10
8 Use We instead of I		12
9 Dry Run Code 4 Practice		13
10 Tactical Breathing		17
11 First Thing to Learn in Edged Weapons Counter Tactics		18
12 Learn to Use a Tourniquet		18
12.1 Edged Weapons Counter Tactics		21
13 Scan Scan Scan		26

14 Use dorky blue gloves instead of tacti-cool black	28
15 "We're not here to hurt you"	29
16 Show me your hands…Maybe	30
17 Be surprised if the suspect isn't in the next room	32
18 Get there safely	33
19 Don't Fuckin' Move	36
20 "I'm not going to tell you again"	39
21 "We're gonna put you in cuffs ok?"	41
22 Control First, Cuff Second	43
23 Water! Water you going to do?	45
24 Light tactics	49
25 More light tactics	51
26 Cuffs On, Knees Off	53
27 Excited Delirium	55
28 You don't have any guns or knives in the car, do you?	57
29 "Tap Rack Ready" after a gun grab	59
30 Contact Shots…not really	61
31 Verbally Searching a Suspect	63

32 "We'll find you a fight kid"   67

33 333   69

34 Physically searching a suspect   71

35 Jits, Judo, Karate, Boxing, Muay Thai   75

36 Give the injured officer work to do   78

37 Give the self-injured suicidal person

    work to do   80

38 Let your toes do the walking   84

39 What's the problem with

    "What's the problem?"   86

40 Officer Involved Shooting…

    get some sleep cycles   89

41 How many rounds did you or your

    partner fire, what exactly was the suspect

    wearing at the time and other

    insignificant questions in a life and

    death match, and other beauties

    of educating non-police people   91

42 Cops on Camera   105

43 Let the neighborhood breathe   108

44 3 Boxes to put your stuff in   117

45 Spot the Difference   118

46 It's a Numbers Game   126

47 The Kids, on Fire   134

48 Perception IS Reality   140

49 "O.K. O.K." and other tricks

   cop killers play   145

50 Don't be an asshole   152

Acknowledgments   154

About the Author   157

QUESTION:

WHAT IF CRIMINALS GET A HOLD OF THIS BOOK AND LEARN ABOUT "OUR" TACTICS? ISNT THAT GIVING AWAY OUR ADVANTAGE?

ANSWER:

GOOD QUESTION. BUT I WOULD RATHER CHANCE THAT LE, SECURITY, AND CORRECTIONS OFFICERS WILL BE READING IT MORE.

IF, HOWEVER, A "BAD GUY" DOES READ THIS, THEN HOPEFULLY PERHAPS HE/SHE WILL REALIZE THAT WE ARE CONSTANTLY TRAINING TO GET BETTER AND BETTER EVERY DAY BY LEARNING HOW TO PREDICT, PREVENT AND WIN VIOLENT ENCOUNTERS.

IM ALSO PRETTY SURE THAT THEY ARE INSTEAD, READING BOOKS AND SEARCHING THE WEB, ON HOW TO COUNTERFEIT CARDS, MAKE DOPE, HIDE DOPE, TRANSPORT DOPE, MAKE GUNS, DESTROY CRIME GUNS, STEAL CARS (PARTS), LAUNDER MONEY, ESCAPE FROM CUFFS ETC. ETC.

THEY, LIKE US, ARE CONSTANTLY EVOLVING. LET'S STAY AHEAD OF THE GAME (WHICH ACTUALLY ISN'T EVEN CLOSE TO A GAME).

FEEL FREE TO USE THE NEXT FEW BLANK PAGES TO MAKE NOTES AS YOU LEARN YOUR CRAFT AT OFFICER SAFETY SEMINARS, CONFERENCES, AND IN-SERVICE TRAINING. KEEP YOUR HANDBOOK HANDY.

BE BETTER THAN YESTERDAY…

*CHECK WITH YOUR DEPARTMENTAL SUBJECT MATTER EXPERTS TO ENSURE THESE TACTICS ALIGN WITH YOUR AGENCY'S BEST PRACTICE METHODS.

Introduction

It is pouring rain outside on a stormy November morning in Delta, British Columbia. What better time to take our Auzzie Shepard (named Hazel/Crazel) for a blast through the muddy trails!

With my favorite pump-up dopamine-releasing tunes blasting in my ears, we take off and let loose. It's pissing cats, and now, dogs! During these "workouts" I often shadow box, bobbing/weaving/slipping (punches, not on the ice) and striking at imaginary opponents and executing foot sweeps, reaps and other takedowns. Changing direction, getting "off the line" and moving in spontaneous directions and fashions is all part of the chaos.

Push-ups and soaking wet sit-ups are included in the deal. The rare trail-sharers with raincoats and umbrellas must think I'm/we're nuts! I don't really give a flying fuche. The more I do it, the more adrenalin surges I get, the louder I scream inside and sometimes outside. The dog loves it as she gazes back laughing and bounding like a kudu gazelle being chased by a lion, albeit an older one!

We naturally feed off of each other's raw instinctive primal energy. The final sprint home gasses me. My heart pounds in my chest and the rising metallic flavor of effort is spat out as white froth and tumbles windswept to the ground. I am ALIVE. I feel good and strong and tell myself "Today I'm gonna start what I have thought about for years. Writing it all down. A book. To help police be safer". And what does all that look like?

This: It's the extra things I talk about/teach to the police recruits during their use of force training. And things I have talked about with the in-service cops when I was in the Officer Safety Section with my prior agency. It's not the blocks and blocks of curriculum of legal studies, traffic rules, invest, human relations, court and patrol procedures. That will save a case, but likely not your or someone else's life in the seconds leading up to, during, or after a critical incident.

It's about the stuff that happens several seconds before, during or after a knife attack; gun fight; ambush; spontaneous empty hand attack; multiple assailants swarming; car chase; speeding vehicle collision etc. It's about recognizing pending violence and the sometimes overt or subtle indicators leading up to it.

It's about increasing your survival skills and preventing exploitation of your weaknesses.

It's about the realities of helping others when they can't help themselves and going home at the end of the night or day or whatever shift you are on.

It's about my almost 30 years of police work learning from others and myself and dealing with situations that are completely fucked up in relation to the mostly everyday things that civilians experience in their daily lives. That's because cops put themselves between the predators and the prey.

I always remind new and old officers that "being a cop doesn't make you any better than anyone else, it just makes you better prepared to deal with situations that others aren't trained to deal with". Plain and Simple.

That's the other thing about this book. It is very plain and simple.

I opted out of having an editor proof it and check for grammar and punctuation and proper use of the English language. Poor sod would be a drunk 2 weeks in! See, I got hired just before the requirements upped to college or university degrees. I just barely made it through grade 12 in 1980! I did however (or should it read "However, I did") take some part-time night classes in community colleges that padded my resume a little bit.

One was a memory course, which the only thing I seem to remember was that the instructor was an asshole and full of himself.

I also backpacked around the world with one of my best friends (Hammy) for 2 years visiting 33 countries and hitting 4 continents. That taught me a whole lot about other people and cultures and a ton about friendship, perseverance, flexibility, patience, simplicity, nature and most importantly, myself and how I relate to others in peace and aggression.

My hat does go off to those that can apply themselves through the rigors of academic studies in ALL vocations.

I'm not that smart but learned some things to keep me relatively street smart, and now want to pass them on to you and your brothers and sisters in what I believe is to be one of the world's most difficult, challenging yet self-rewarding professions. That's how this book will read. Plain and Simple. Like Life and Death. Either you are alive, or you are dead.

I dearly hope that by sharing these tips, law enforcement officers will be safer. And their families, friends, sisters, and brothers in blue, as well as the citizens who support them will not have to mourn more loss.

    Let's begin…

50 Tactical Tips

#1 "I'm not going back to jail"

If you hear these words from a suspect you are dealing with, take heed. This is very different than somebody saying "I can't go to jail today…because I have to work, catch a flight, school" or other *fill in the blank* reason. That is an attempt to plead or debate the pending arrest.

The person who states "I am NOT going to (back to) jail" is clearly telling you they may do whatever it takes to *not* be arrested which could include serious injury or death to you or them. It is a statement.

One such fellow we encountered on January 2nd, 1991, was named Kenneth H. He had escaped from a penitentiary and had been robbing banks and stores over the Christmas season (receiving not giving). When we challenged him, he drew and pointed a loaded 9mm Luger (which he had used to shoot at a bank witness days before). At the inquest into his death, his ex-wife testified that he had contacted her while on the run. She tried to convince him to turn himself in as his drug-fueled violent behavior was escalating and making the news. She stated he told her "I'm not going back to jail". He was right. More to follow on that encounter as there were many lessons learned that day.

#2 Visible Handcuff Key

I thought a good title for this book would also have been Tactical Empathy. Sounds a little soft but I actually mean it as in "put yourself in the bad guy's shoes". What would *you* do if you were the asocial predator who has been arrested by the police and needed to escape the jail detention and/or upcoming likely prison term?

One of the key things (pardon the pun) would be to see where the cuff key was on the officer so that after I trip them up, then smash my foot into their neck/head etc., I could locate the key immediately instead of not knowing and fumbling around through pockets with handcuffs on (back or front) and escape. Fumbling around all takes time. And that relates to time to get seen/reported by witnesses, caught by other cops etc.

When I worked the jail for the mandatory 6 months of inside time as a rookie, I also openly wore the big old jail cell key (as others did) as a sign of coolness and the "Look at me now, I'm in charge!" I'm really lucky I didn't get dummied for it. I see too many cops wearing handcuff keys on their duty belts which are like shiny lures to dangerous hungry predator sharks.

Sometimes officers even have them on a retractable lanyard which would make it even easier to grab and use. Put them in a deep pocket. It is about the only piece of equipment that you never need in an emergency.

Things have generally slowed down after the cuffs are on so double locking isn't a speed required response. Similarly, when releasing a suspect, urgency and speed to de-cuff is not the priority.

#3 "You Don't Have any Knives Guns or Hand Grenades on you, do you?"

This one drives me nuts. It also cost an officer his life, so don't ever use it. I admit I have said it and heard it during my younger years. Sometimes we want to lighten things up during an arrest/detention/street check to keep the tensions low and not piss people off or start conflict. Prior to, or during an uncuffed pat down frisk (more on that later) or search, officers would say to the suspect "You don't have any knives, guns or hand grenades on you, do you?" On the rarest of occasions people *are* carrying explosives but for the most part they aren't. When this line is used it provides the subject an easy comfortable denial and verbal out with the often-relieved smiley-faced answer of "Hahahah…NO"!

Unfortunately for one officer, the suspect had a .22 in his waistband which he accessed and killed the officer with shortly after he was "offered" the verbal out. The subject did not have any prior criminal record but felt the small amount of marijuana on him would send him to jail and his life was spiraling down.

A better question is plain and simple. "Do you have any weapons on you?" If the subject pauses/stalls or says, "What do you mean?" or "Huh?" or "Like what?" those are all good verbal danger cues to take notice of. Sometimes when asked, suspects will glance at where it is as their brain tries to come up with responses. Watch for the cues. Communication is largely body language under stress. More of that to follow including "facial grooming" prior to an attack.

#4 Kicking Guns and Knives out of hands after an Officer Involved Shooting

After a suspect has been shot and incapacitated there is usually no immediate need to rush in and disarm them of a weapon. They just tried (albeit unsuccessfully) to kill you with it, I'm sure they would love another chance. If you get too close, they may be feigning unconsciousness, or regain consciousness, and attempt another slash/shot etc. Kind of like an injured fallen grizzly bear. Still dangerous just not as mobile. Think AIM: Ability. Intent. Means. Also remember Force Sciences™ Action vs. Reaction Time Experiment.

Medics are coming, let the dust and other microbials settle and take a big inhale exhale and ask yourself "If I was the bad guy, where would I want the cop(s) to move to?" and if the answer is "closer to me so I can hurt them", then don't. Make sure you aren't getting played. First Safety, *then* First Aid.

I once wrote a related Use of Force Opinion Report regarding an OIS. Long story short, the suspect was sleeping in his minivan 2 days after the attempted murder of his landlord and the shooting death of a couple in a sushi restaurant.

The SWAT Bearcat rammed him almost into a ditch. He climbed out the window in his underwear and started ripping rounds from his rifle at the team. They shot him. He fell down on the gravel road, long gun by his feet looking pretty much incapacitated. The members started approaching at which time he reached out with his foot (probably to try to bring the gun back to him). His toe was enough to press the trigger and a .30-06 round cranked off into a farmer's field thankfully not hitting anyone. WTF! Great goal-oriented, never give-up mentality, but for the wrong team. Subject died on scene. No officer injured. My saying…"Wait, Don't Take The Bait!"

#5 Too Many Yellers Spoil the High-Risk Arrest/Takedown

In the event where 2 or more officers are involved in a high-risk arrest/takedown, it is best if only one cop does the verbal commands/instructions etc.

For example, 5 cops bust through a door (no knock if you still are allowed or warrant execution etc.). One SWAT cop yells "Don't Move" the other came from a recent course and yells "Get on the Ground" (thinking higher the threat the lower they go, which is pretty good, if everyone is on the same page). The accompanying neighboring officer commands the subject to "Turn Around", the Detective who swore the affidavit and is along for the ride says something like "Hands up" or "Lift your shirt up" (not a fan of the last one TBH).

The suspect turns around and gets shot. In the after-action investigation, one officer states he said, "Get on the Ground", the other says "Ohhhh, I said turn around". Kinda sounds the same but is confusing in the heat of the moment and is risky for everyone there. One Cop, One Job. LOUD CLEAR SIMPLE REPETITIVE PROFESSIONAL VERBAL COMMANDS but never "I'm not going to tell you again!" …which I will tell you again… in Tip #20.

#6 Brake Lights Stay On… Beware

This one is very concerning. Over the decades I have reviewed hundreds of OIS's where the suspect(s) was pulled over in a vehicle. In an inordinate (trying to use big smart word here) number of times, the bright red brake lights remain on as the officer(s) walks up to the car/truck. The suspect then opens fire when the officer gets to the door and the suspect then takes off.

In a normal violator pull over, the driver usually puts the vehicle in park. The common sequence of lighting is: Brake lights on, white light to rear (as the shifter passes reverse), then brake lights off when car is in park (or N with hand brake on in manual shift vehicles). The running lights are then the only ones on, except maybe for a 4-way flasher or turn signal.

I brought this up with some executives with the Force Science Research Institute (great courses BTW) and also at some Street Survival Seminar Conferences (also good think tanks and road trips). The only reason we could come up with is that the suspect is likely so focused on the pending attempted murder that he or she (but he in most cases) isn't thinking perfectly straight. There is a LOT of human aggression and risk/threats building, and the stress drive overrides the "normal" behavior practices. In some cases, they leave the car in gear with the brakes applied simply to make a speedy escape once the officer begins their approach on foot. My reminder: "Fully Red, Might Want you Dead" or "Brake Lights Stay on…might be a Con!"

#7 License and Registration Please

For years police have been pulling cars over and asking the driver for "License and Registration" in the same sentence. Most of the time it's not a problem. However, it can provide an opportunity for the occupant(s) to get the jump on the officer.

Here's why: If you ask for both at the same time, it gives someone the opportunity to reach into several places with little assuredness of what they will produce or where their hand(s) is/are going. Particularly if there is a passenger in the car, then he may reach into the glove box while the driver reaches into the console/or jacket. It is really hard to effectively watch four hands at one time. Better yet, start with one question at a time and wait for the response:

Question #1. "Sir/Ma'am, do you have a valid driver's license?" They will respond with either a Yes or a No. If it's "No", then there is no reason for them to be reaching for anything yet until you ask for a wallet I.D. etc. If they answer "Yes", then ask them question #2.

Question # 2. "Do you have it with you today and if so, where is it in the car?" They should be steered (pardon the pun) to answer the question first. Then you can track their hands to it. If the answer is yes but not with them then you can ask for ID and begin the identity finding questions. Once you have the DL in hand, then you can act surprised as if you forgot and ask this next step.

Question # 3 "Oh yeah! Do you have the insurance papers in the car and if so, where are they?" They will respond with either yes "in the glove box, console, visor" etc. and you can track their hands to it. If they say they don't know, then the car may not be lawfully theirs or borrowed etc.

The general theme here is ask separately and slow it down which will give you time to read subversive behaviors (more on what that looks like later) both physically and verbally.

#8 Use We instead of I

Kind of blended with the above vehicle stop tactics. It's better to say to the violator "The reason *we* stopped you is because you're going 70 miles an hour in a 50 mile an hour zone" or "For not wearing a seatbelt" etc. Hopefully when you use the word "we" it creates the illusion that there is another officer nearby. Maybe in the car, maybe that person on the sidewalk etc.

It's an old military trick that when the enemy was looking through binoculars at the opposing soldiers on the horizon/berm/hilltop etc. the soldiers would run down the covered side and then reappear with a different flag going the other direction and put hats on/off changing appearance at a distance. The scout would then mistakenly report to command that there were at least 100 when there were a lot less.

It creates a defensive hesitant mind when they think there is more opposition. Keep them guessing. Martial arts of the mind and the mouth and Psy-ops!

#9 Dry Run Code 4 Practice

Preparing yourself for a high intensity event and being able to broadcast the information clearly, concisely, and calmly is easy to do…with a little practice!

I used to drive into work and pretend that a vehicle in front of me had just been involved in a hit and run, robbery, drive by etc. I would immediately glance at my street signs for the location and get on the air (pretending to grab a mic in my own car) and say "4Charlie51 Code 4" (or whatever district I was travelling in). Then I would wait for the "dispatcher" to say "4C51 go ahead". Then I would actually speak out loud in my calmest voice stating "4C51, I just witnessed a (fill in the blank), 41st and Oak northbound, plate when you're ready". I would *hear* the CD say "Go". Then I would actually look and call out the license plate and actual description of the car driving in-front of me "Charlie Papa Xray 7-5-9 on a white Honda minivan. Still northbound through 37th, normal speed.

My scenario would go on for as long as I needed to get into it. (I'm not detouring from work if they do)! What it created was a blueprint for performing under a "simulated" level of stress requiring cognitive processing and communication. I actually felt my heartrate increase and then practiced breathing tactics to stay chill and reverse the effect. The tone of my voice would drop as the pressure on the vocal cords relaxed as opposed to increased pressure and resultant high pitched squeaky voice. I would call out added observations like "A gun was just thrown out the passenger window into the Shell gas station at 25th" or "The suspect vehicle just collided with a pole at X intersection, driver out running northbound, description when you're ready" etc.

Well guess what happened during a patrol night shift? A robbery pointer vehicle was broadcast on another channel reporting that a suspect just held up a Subway sandwich store and left in a tan 4-door Toyota on file as stolen. The subsequent information (that later turned out to be unrelated) was that the suspect may be Jules S. (a hang-around back then with the local HA).

I headed over to the area of their clubhouse on Georgia Street. A few minutes later I saw a possible and caught the plate as it rolled up to a fresh red on Hastings Street on Boundary Rd. Same plate! Love it!

I took a deep slow nasal inhale, got on the air, and said "2C51 Code 4" and it played out just like in my "training". He proceeded northbound and then into a neighboring jurisdiction. Not speeding. Quite normal driving indicating turns too (stressed out or super calm dangerous aware suspect).

Heading into an industrial area (by the grain towers) was a little suspy so I was preparing for an ambush or a dump (car not me). He sped up, I lit it up (marked car) and we were off to the races Code 4 (ironically beside Hastings Horserace Course, cheesy but super fun place). Other cars joined in. Giddy Up!

This one pursuit lasted about 10 minutes. Ahh the good old days. *Pursuits are an extreme hazard and are like rolling 10 pairs of dice at once, so know your agency policies and make sure it is absolutely critical that the engagement is necessary. Don't change yours or your partner's (or others) lives unless lives depend on it. Now, back to the story:

He ended up crashing down a 50-foot embankment. Car empty upon inspection. Suspect fled in dark ravine. Like a scene from Fugitive starring Harrison Ford. Driver's door open, windshield wipers click clacking back and forth. Dogs and SWAT arrested him 45 minutes later hiding by a house on a hill next to the ravine.

Had a slew of warrants out for him. Fun fact, it wasn't the associate! Weird how some things just happen and are coincidental.

A few days later a squad mate (Big Mikey) suggested I pull the tapes 'cause he said the whole thing was so calm it sounded like I was reading a bedtime story to my kids called Goodnight Moon!

Good Practice make Better Performance. BTW I was

shitting myself at several points, but one apparently couldn't tell by my voice! "Goodnight Goon! Have a nice sleep in the crowbar hotel".

#10 Tactical Breathing

Combat or tactical breathing is a way for police officers to maintain control of their breathing respirations and therefore heart rate under stress. If the brain is perfused with oxygenated blood, it makes it easier to make good decisions and positively affect the fine and complex motor skills such as drawing and using a firearm and other critical tasks during an encounter. A simple method for performing the combat breathing exercise is to inhale through the nose for four seconds. The next stage is to hold the breath for four more seconds. The next step is to slowly exhale the breath (like making a candle flicker pace) and then hold for four more seconds.

Simply repeat this process for four cycles or however much time you have. You will have positively reduced your heart rate and can make better cognitive choices/actions/decisions and stay safer (and lose less blood if that's an issue). This is a widely known tactic with many different names (Combat Breathing, Autogenic, Box Breathing Chill Brah! etc.). It can also be used if you begin to recognize you or another officer becoming agitated. The old saying of "Take a breath" should now be "Hey partner, take 4 breaths 4 times!"

#11 First Thing to Learn in Edged Weapons Counter Tactics

(See Following Tip)!

#12 Learn to Use a Tourniquet

The first thing we teach the recruits before they learn how to counter an edged weapon attack is how to attenuate a critical bleed to the arms/legs/neck.

There are several excellent life-saving TK's on the market. Research the legit ones. Practice applying to yourself with one hand only*. *With that in mind, avoid securing the stowed TK with the Velcro™ white or other colored tab "locked in place". It makes it extra difficult to do a one-handed application. Back the securing tab off on the same side or along the TK belt. Then practice, practice, practice.

Having 2 hands is a luxury when putting on yourself or others. Also, when "loading it" avoid weaving the free end thru 2 buckle slots. Leave that for when it's on the limb and you have the dexterity or time if even at all (there is way too much Velcro™ war going on which takes precious seconds away from stopping the bleeding).

Finally, no matter where the wound site, take it as high up the arm/leg as possible to where the muscles taper and the arteries are better accessed. Make sure there isn't anything in the cargo pants pockets like notebooks, gloves, tins of cha etc. that would make the TK not bear down on the tissue/arteries. Secure the loose end so it doesn't get caught in car/helo doors or caught up on foliage/fences etc.

We began training and issuing TK's as part of a department-wide initiative. Wait. Prior to that we approached an Inspector (now retired thankfully) who denied our first request to purchase 500 units to roll out to patrol. He said it was too expensive and not really practicable. Also wanted a formal business case report (like we knew how to do that!).

So back then we had 2 studs (Paramedic III Brian Twaites and VGH ER doctor Eric Vu) teach us how to teach cops how to apply a makeshift TK from a duty baton and hobble restraint strap or any other at hand kit. That info actually saved a victim from a gang shooting when the officer arrived on scene and used her baton and a passerby's macrame belt! Way to go Cst. Cho!

Since the new way-better Inspector said go for it, there have been too many saves to count. Including a member who was shooting at the range off-duty and blasted his leg. He had his TK mollied to his backpack and he slapped it on his leg and saved his own life. Preparedness Practice and Mindset. Great guy, Great piece of kit. Get some!

Tactical Consideration:

Most Combat TK's are black (with white or grey securing

tab). This could pose a problem if trying to find it in low light. Most uniforms are dark as well which might make it difficult if it's not in a standard location agency-wide. Or perhaps you are assisting another jurisdiction and they carry somewhere else. Bright (but not reflective) TK's may be easier to see and hence locate. Seconds count in stopping blood loss. (Thanks, Big Frankie!). Injury to neck: Press 3 fingers and try to occlude the artery. The other artery provides oxygen to the brain. The body is pretty awesomely designed. Thx Designer!

#12.1 Edged Weapons Counter Tactics

First off, why are so many people fighting on counters? (John Irving Esq. III).

Secondly, but also seriously firstly, have a plan in place which translates to practicing a solid foundational tactic that allows you to not just survive, but win a knife (or any other edged weapon) attack. Which I will call an EWA. There are generally two types of attacks: Anticipated, where there is info or observations from distance; and Unanticipated, where it is without any warning. We will focus on the latter here.

If a "technique" is complex in its application (requiring time to process and source answers) there is no problem if the user has that time to work with. Think of a complex algebraic exam question (not that I did any) in which the student has 20 minutes to solve. Yes, the stress of failure (embarrassment, rejection, non-promotion to next class) may be looming but the actual physical harm isn't present. The student can try solving from different formula applications using creativity, memory or trial and error until a solution is decided upon.

Under life or death or serious injury threat, we don't have enough actual time to employ such super technical or thoughtful solves.

Therefore, the type of strategies we need in a spontaneous EWA should be simple (like the name EWA) in concept and principle, and simple to activate (basic, gross motor delivery fast-fire responses). Kind of thoughtless really.

Things that have been, or should be driven into officers in training sessions, so that they buy time and conversely don't lose time in reacting to an EWA.

Such things as: Maintaining a "field interview" or better defined as "reactionary gap". Giving you a chance to react by having distance which buys you time. Usually in "normal" human proxemics, about 2 outstretched arms lengths away. This is, if you and the subject reached out an arm, the fingertips would meet in the middle (ET Phone Home!). The next skill set will be to recognize pending attack cues (see multiple tips in book) and therefore be a hard target. That also means tactical positioning from the outset, shielding, distance, re-evaluating, and moving off the line of attack if possible if/when feces is about to hit the spinning blade.

Note: Most people are right-handed. The three common attack lines/angles and grips are:

Thrust/Stab

This is where the suspect either grabs or holds the officer with one hand and attacks with the knife like a piston (forward and reset back and forward again). Torso is a common target when face-to-face standing.

Ice Pick

This is where the suspect holds the knife grip so that the tip points downward. The action is from above and again piston like or circular in motion. Neck and shoulder are common targets when standing face to face or prone.

Side to Side Slashing

This where the suspect "wands" the knife left and right back and forth in front of them. Common target would naturally be hands and arms or stomach but can vary if elevation changes.

Whichever style the suspect uses, it is important to interrupt the delivery of the primary and/or the multiple strike attack.

Changing locations, albeit in close quarters, confuses the suspect and they have to retract and reset to find their target (experiencing their own OODA Loop). In that fraction of a second, if it's possible, arm yourself and shoot the suspect from an unconventional platform. Most likely one-handed point and press while still moving and rinse and repeat as necessary. Then proceed to call resources and manage any damage with distance, shielding and self-care. Another good reason not to rush in right away and try any fancy knife disarms.

Those seemingly cool techniques are simply parlor tricks to inflate egos and impress audiences and work spectacularly well when performed with a complicit training buddy, a well-lit training club with 2 ¼ inch poly mats, no recently smoked coke or meth and a dulled training blade (although I must say, there are some most excellent realistic safe training knives out there)!!! Insert Shameless PLUG here!

If body movement (Tai Sabaki, in martial arts) and CQB avoidance isn't feasible, then another consideration is to try to isolate the arm (delivery limb) which holds the weapon. Don't chase the hand/knife. The weapon hand moves fast, the elbow a little slower and the upper arm the slowest. If you are able to glom onto the entire arm (solid elbow control and minimize reset ability by trapping), then with your other hand deliver immediate catastrophic deadly force strikes to viable targets. Blasting the side of the neck, base of skull, or the throat, will likely create a window of opportunity allowing yourself to access your firearm or disengage. Strikes need to be delivered with maximum power and speed and include as much body weight through the targets as possible.

Force (F) = m x a.

The open web of your free hand is a great tool to strike the throat with. Competitive sports punches can average about 70olbs of force. Average people can punch 300lbs. Putting as much of that into the trachea (flexible but delicate structure) will likely cause a primal response from the attacker who will instinctively shield and hopefully go from predator mind to prey mind.

Punching with closed fist knuckles runs the risk of breaking your own hand/wrist which could affect the ability to access your firearm or other items (radio/tourniquet). Using hammer fists/forearms to base of skull, side of neck is a lot safer and more powerful in a primal way.

The key to training these responses is to practice practice practice. Slowly to begin with, working up to full speed blind drills ("Turnaround and begin"). Hundreds of reps. Doesn't take too long in the grand scheme of things.

What's also important is to have your role player deliver a repeated, cyclical in nature, attack pattern. All of the above attack patterns repeat themselves in a cluster. These patterns will then be recognized by the officer as edged weapon attacks instead of standard punches/assaultive behavior. Repeating the cycle effect will create blueprints for proper responses. It is critical to train in surviving and winning ambushes (whether the subject is armed or not). Tony Blauer explains it so very well in his research and findings and simple but effective tactics.

#13 Scan Scan Scan

Quite often during an officer involved shooting, members are so focused on the person they just shot that they forget to look around and ensure there is not a second, third, or maybe even a fourth suspect present or innocent that needs help.

For example, during an armed robbery that the officer responds to (or happens upon), he or she is confronted by the suspect and has to shoot. The officer moves to a better place and tells the suspect "Don't move. Help is on the way" after they have summoned resources. The problem is that this person may not be alone in their crime spree. There may be a wheel man or wheel woman who comes into the store when they heard the shooting, and the officer can be blindsided.

There are two general facial expressions that you need to recognize:

One is shock and awe from the overwhelming stress. That would be, for example, the shopkeeper or a witness. Their facial expression is usually a circular open mouth to intake air to oxygenate the brain to help process the event or fuel the muscles for flight.

Their eyes are usually open wide and circular, again to take in as much light and therefore information as they try to figure out what the Hell to do. Sometimes their hands are placed up to their head to support the frontal cortex logic decision process. This face is generally not a face that needs to be dealt with as a threat. Perhaps they need to be told to go back inside their house, move away from the burning car or whatever situation they're overwhelmed with.

The face the officer needs to recognize most is one called "contempt". Contempt appears as a tightened mouth, squinted eyes, looking through eyebrows, gritting teeth and almost looks like a grimace. The body will also be in a C-shaped predator forward-spine mode as opposed to standing erect or bent backwards (like the shocked witness mentioned above).

If the officer recognizes somebody at the scene with a contempt face and body language, they likely need to be dealt with or at least addressed. Perhaps this is the friend or gang associate of the suspect that the officers just shot. This person is possibly a threat, and they need to be commanded probably to the floor and then processed safely as they maybe are in protection/rescue mode for their buddy.

The common training saying of "Ground and Look Around" applies whether you foot swept or took the subject to the ground or shot someone making them fall. Don't just do the classis range scan (blurry left and right to appease the instructor and pass the qual). Actually, look at and read faces and body language.

#14 Use dorky blue gloves instead of tacti-cool black

If you're dealing with a suspect or a victim that has a wound and there's blood leaving the wound, and you have time, it is best practice to put on some medical grade gloves (universal precaution). The unfortunate thing for police is that we often think that black gloves are better. The real answer is they're not. There are several reasons not to wear black gloves. If you are doing a self wet-check after a shooting and or stabbing, you may misinterpret moisture such as rain or even sweat as blood. Yes, it is not tacti-cool, but it's practi-cool if you wear a blue glove.

That way, blood will be easier to see when you are sourcing out an injury site. Or, in particular, looking which limb you need to maybe put a TK on.

However, black is better for particulate drugs if you are searching a home and/or a vehicle because it's easier to see powder residue on the black glove. But if the suspect pops out and a shooting happens, then…hmmmm, maybe one blue one black? Could be Trendy! Next Level Shit!

#15 "We're not here to hurt you"

For many years, the standard police patter when dealing with a subject who is resisting or non-compliant was to continually yell "Stop resisting". Although it somewhat tells the subject what to do, it can be misinterpreted by others and also other police.

It is better to be specific when using police commands during an arrest and control situation such as: "Put your other hand behind your back". "Stop holding onto the steering wheel". "Let go of the fence" etc. etc.

An even better line of dialogue when dealing with a subject is to start off saying (if time permits) "We are not here to hurt you". First of all, of course you'll identify yourself as the police. But when you say, "We're not here to hurt you", the suspect and also the competing audience hears that as well. This puts the ball in the other person's court as to whether you have to escalate and/or use force or not. And it also lets the subject know you are looking after them so they hopefully will not be so reactive. If a person is in crisis, they are likely scared and confused.

YELLING DOESN'T HELP CALM PEOPLE DOWN! See what I mean?

#16 "Show me your hands"…Maybe

Depending upon the situation, it may not be tactical to tell somebody to immediately take their hands out of their pockets.

For example, if you encounter a person who matches the description of a suspect who just robbed a corner store or perhaps threatened somebody with a knife and you come up on them to find their hands in their pockets, it is a good tactic to tell them (at gunpoint and shielding) "Keep your hands in your pockets". And then tell them that they match the description of a subject involved in X. If they start to draw their hand out of their pocket, then this should send alarm bells that they may be presenting the knife/weapon.

You could go further and say "Police. Don't move". "Keep your hands in your pockets". When/if they ask "Why?" Simply tell them "Because you match the description of somebody who may have a knife. If you have a knife in your pocket, it's not a big deal right now. Leave it in your pocket. Which pocket is it in? O.K. Slowly take your hand out of your pocket. Now take the other hand out of your other pocket and lay down on the ground. Do not reach for the knife or you will be shot" etc. etc. These are very clear standing/lying down orders. And police then have a framework to follow.

If you ask them to show their hands right of the bat, then that gives them an opportunity to draw whatever it is from their pockets. Perhaps it is a gun. It is better to keep their hands in their pockets while moving to a better place. This gives you a chance to come up with a plan to deal with the *believed to be* armed subject.

The higher the threat, the lower they go. If you find them with their hands out of their pockets and you believe they have a weapon secreted in the pocket then it's perfectly good to say, "Keep your hands in view. Do not reach for any of your pockets". "It's not a big deal if you have a weapon, but it's a big deal if you reach for it or take it out". Setting clear context allows everybody to understand what your concern is.

17 Be surprised if the suspect *isn't* in the next room

It is important to have the mindset that when searching a house or a building, that you are *not* surprised by somebody you find who was hiding around a corner, under a bed or in a closet etc.

The mindset trick is to be surprised if they're *not* behind the door. That way you will be less likely to have a startle response when you encounter them 'cause you were looking for them and expecting them to be there! So be the predator, not the prey.

18 Get there safely

A great percentage of Line of Duty Deaths (LODD) and injuries occur by the simple fact of where officers work (in and around vehicles). Getting out on roadways to check drivers. Driving to and from calls (code 3 or not), parked while writing tickets/citations/crim record checks/computer work or as a result of vehicular collisions (single or multiple).

Therefore, always wear your seat belt, even if you're going slowly and patrolling perhaps the back lane of a high drug-use neighborhood.

A lot of officers would say "But I need my seatbelt off because I need to get in and out of the car quickly". Yes and No. The problem with that is as your car proceeds out of the mouth of the lane, a Five S's car (Speeding, Stoned, Stolen, Stupid or Shitty driver) collides with you. Even though you were just going 5 or 10 miles per hour the other vehicle was travelling at a higher rate. Science/Physics takes care of the rest. The Kinetic Energy of a vehicle travelling 20mph is approximately 200,000 Joules*.

The other excuse that officers don't wear seatbelts is because of potential ambushes. There absolutely have been some ambushes while police officers are seated in their vehicles. But by far, the vast percentage of injuries and death are from collisions.

Practice drawing from a seated position. Also practice getting out of the bullet trap and move to a better place of cover and concealment. Fight back fast and smart. Be a hard target.

It is also important while driving around on patrol to keep the driver's side and/or the passenger side window cracked an inch. This allows you to hear ambient noise. It may be a vehicle accelerating through some traffic lights. It could be the sound of screeching brakes, or perhaps even a pedestrian yelling "Stop" as a child runs out from between two parked cars chasing a ball.

Another good tactic to "get there safely" is don't go too fast (hard I know but…). That means don't speed so excessively that you are out of control and T-bone a citizen or another police car who is doing the same thing at the intersection. If you are in a collision, you will deplete resources that were going to the first call of service as cover, and have to deal with injuring another cop (almost like a blue on blue but black and white on black and white).

Get there quickly but safely and you're better able to help everyone including the victim, yourself, and your partner.

*One of the most popular measured explosive compounds is TNT (trinitrotoluene). The energy released in an explosion of 1 gram of TNT is approximately 4000 Joules. Speeding car at

80mph = 800,000 Joules plus.

Driving fast is a "rush" but don't be in a rush. I've been the primary vehicle in dozens of pursuits. Some real doozies! Lock on is natural but it can turn into a significant gong show in a matter of seconds.

Also, due to the massive litigious nature of LE these days, try to mitigate being hung out to dry. Tough decisions to make. Don't allow Ego to dominate the predator drive literally and figuratively. Let's maybe explore launching pursuit drones, utilize air and ground support and containment and K9 at the inevitable destination dump and run.

#19 Don't Fuckin' Move

The first person we have to control in a use of force event is ourselves.

Try to stay away from using profanity because it appears that you have lost control and may appear angry and unprofessional, and lawyers can run with it easier against you. Keep reading this fucking book. It's good shit. Point well taken? "Anger is one letter away from Danger" (Sgt. Johnny Roberts's quote) ...or so he claims!

Over the last 20 years I have written hundreds of use of force opinions ranging from: Internal Affairs, OIS, UOF, Coroners Court, Supreme Court etc. Most, thankfully, have exonerated officers from the issues surrounding their of use of force.

A handful have determined that the officer's actions were not consistent with their training or what an officer with reasonable experience would have done if they were presented with the similar situation, and therefore found to be excessive in the trier of facts conclusion.

In almost all of those ones, evidence was discovered that the officer was acting in a punitive fashion and was invested in an EGO battle (tough guy, bully, jackass etc.). *Side note: those guys are usually the ones that are not confident or competent in physical skills and combatives...funny that…"All show and no go!" Another chapter…maybe.

In a local case, an officer had responded to a 911 call from a woman who was walking in the park with her family. She noticed a guy passed out in a crappy pickup truck with empty booze bottles on the ground. The officer showed up and woke him up. Plastered. The officer opened the door and dragged him to the ground (ok, not too bad) but then stood him back up without handcuffing (Wait. What?).

The guy could hardly stand balanced, save for holding onto the driverside mirror. Dude wobbled around some more and talked some "shit" back (No threats, just typical drunk drivel).

The officer pushed him onto and off the hood of the truck (rag doll) for about 10 seconds then sharply pulled his head backwards and threw him to the ground (uncontrolled) causing him to smack the back of his melon on the gravel lot. Dude was out cold.

The lady (who later stated in evidence that she was filming this to help the officer if it went out of control 'cause she likes police) yelled out "Hey, whooooa, that's not necessary!" "I am the one who called 911!" "What are you doing?". The officer looked up surprised (go figure) and yelled back at her saying "You don't know what's going on here. Mind your own business. You don't have to deal with <u>fucking retards</u> like this all the time". Officer charged with assault. Civil Trial concluded. $$$ undisclosed amount to buddy. New Dodge Ram likely!

P.S. Thankfully I don't find those conclusions much. Most cops do great work all of the time, most of the time unnoticed. Some cops shouldn't be public servants period. Or need anger mgmt. re-assignment, training, counselling etc. blah blah blah.

2023 Recruiting Door Sign: **Bullies need not apply**

#20 "I'm not going to tell you again"

When officers are giving commands for people to do something (supported by law) and the subject doesn't comply, some will say as an ultimatum, "I'm not going to tell you again, get out of the car". Then guess what? Buddy doesn't comply and the officer says, "Get out of the car" and the dude says in his mind or out loud "Ha Ha, you said you weren't going to tell me again" and so it begins. A battle of wits or lack thereof. It becomes super frustrating and embarrassing and is usually followed by exasperation and profanity to turn up the intent. "I'm not going to tell you again…Get out of the FUCKING car…NOW!" Of course, dude has an audience and is acting like a petulant 10-year-old child because guess what? That's probably how he's been spoken to before by mom or dad. NO respect. No consequences. Maybe pops finally snapped and smacked him upside the head. No money from pops. Just more hate. But likely from the PD…dollar bills and heat. Don't play their game. Introduce them to the real you. The Contact Professional: "Sir, this is the XPD. You are under arrest. We are not here to hurt you. We are investigating a _____ call. You are a suspect. If you fail to step out of the car voluntarily you will also be charged with obstructing a criminal investigation. For the safety of the public we need you out of the car."

The ball is now clearly in his court. If he says no, go get him or send in the land shark if the risk meets the threshold. Reasonable Dialogue? Check. Escalation based upon subject behavior and non-compliance? Check. No Ego? Check. Granted you could try some Verbal Judo™ and hear him out if tactically feasible. But no more empty threats or punitive looking force. Leave that for the shitty parent. And for Heaven's sake, no more "I'm not going to tell you again!" …Sorry, I didn't mean to tell you again.

Sometimes you hear officers yelling, and I mean yelling, the same command over and over. This is commonly known as the "Goofy Loop". The officer keeps yelling over and over "Get on your stomach. GET on YOUR stomach. GET ON YOUR STOMACH!" Or, "Drop the knife, Drop the knife DROP THE KNIFE, DROP THE KNIFE". The problem with the loop is that it feels like the only active thing to do, and it glues the officer into repetition. The cycle needs to be trained out of officers. This comes from providing information about the risks and recognizing when one is in cycle and how to step out of it. In a training scenario, that is a good time for the instructor to calmly whisper into the trainee's ear, and simply say "It looks like he's not dropping the knife, what would be a better thing to say or do?". With that quiet mental break, they can then better tactically assess the situation and come up with reasonable options to solve the problem.

#21 "We're gonna put you in cuffs ok?" (Compliant Subject)

When arresting a compliant (at least appearing to be compliant) subject, it's not a bad idea to tell them that they will be handcuffed. I'd much rather know, or at least get a feeling, that the SOC is going to resist before I move in to handcuff than while in close proximity.

Here's the scenario:

Subject is believed to have a warrant, or is the suspect in a crime and is not posturing violence. Officer has field interview distance/reaction time.

Police. "You are under arrest for X. We're not here to hurt you. What's your name?"

SOC: "Mike".

Officer: "O.K. Mike, turn around and place your hands behind your back. Do not reach into your waistband or pockets, o.k.?"

Mike complies.

Before control lock or whatever you use as first contact physical hand/arm/wrist control say "Hey Mike, we're gonna cuff you. Don't move, you're doin' great"

Why all this convo?

Fact: Most officers are assaulted on first touch. Why? Simple.

First: The actual physical space is closer than with the field interview (reactionary gap) dialogue distance so it's easier to punch and hit you when closer, *obviously*.

Second: Most people don't like to be touched so they react. Some people flinch on touch or realize that they are actually going to jail etc. so they resist because their world is going for a dump. Some crooks feign compliance. More on that deception and body language and verbal tells later.

Third: If this does turn into a use of force event, then the body cam/audio and also the people filming or close by will be good evidence/witnesses that you reasonably explained to the SOC and set the stage and it was the SOC that resisted when the officer CLEARLY told them not to. Mitigates complaints and liability…(ewww the L word, sorry).

If Mike responds to the earlier dialogue of "Hey Mike, we're gonna cuff you" with "Why?" "This is bullshit!" "But it wasn't me" etc. etc. then you may have prevented a close quarter fight for control. Now you can engage in good persuasion for compliance or escalate to implied tools to generate compliance and prepare mentally and physically for a scrap. Oh, and if he runs, then you are fit and fast and have radios…and K9. *Dollars to doughnuts, if this dude ran, then he likely would have punched you on contact and then ran.

22 Control First, Cuff Second

So many times (especially evident with video on social media) officers are trying to fight and cuff at the same time. The biggest problem with that is the officer loses the ability to use their hand for gripping, twisting, stappling, striking with maximal power etc. So essentially fighting with only one hand in the game (not a game BTW). That's tough. Also, cuffs usually end up falling out of the hand and ending up on the ground. One is none, two is one (another tip later on flashlights!).

The best time to cuff is when you have control. That is generally when the subject is pinned and their fighting spirit feels broken. Some might fake that, so don't be in a rush. Establish good control (low flat heavy). Dialogue is something like: "It's the police". "You're under arrest". "Fights over bud, put your other hand behind your back". "We're not here to hurt you" etc.

Whichever position you are in, don't let the pressure off until they are mechanically restrained. Maybe prone? Then slide up to get the locked-out limb then cuff, or supine, belly to belly, active toes using friction, locks and blocks on hips/shoulders, use a double overhand grip on one arm and effect the "shelf turnover" (great transition taught by Gracie Survival Tactics™ for Law Enforcement)!

Whatever the control, cuff after, not during a struggle/fight.

By the way, the simple reason that officers try to cuff during a fight is that their brain wants the SOC to be cuffed so their motor programs are racing one step ahead of the actual time frames or, they had lousy training. Cuffs Away, Less Problems Today. (Yes, that's mine)!

#23 Water! Water you going to do?

The hardest training course I ever went on was hosted at the Washington State Patrol Academy. It was called Water Combatives and was all about working in and around a waterborne environment (thanks Dave Young)! Four days of grueling pool work, fighting, drown proofing, rescuing, and then the open water swim and gun fight around a boat. Jeepers! However, it was extremely valuable information to come back and share (minus the week-later pneumonia)!

Officers are tasked with working around lakes, streams, rivers, oceans, pools, reservoirs etc. but rarely get training on the risks and tactics. The biggest takeaway which dumbfounded me (not a hard task) was what to do if you fell or were pushed or tackled into the water while wearing FULL duty uniform and kit.

Pond…er that for a moment (sorry)! What would you do? The natural conclusion is to start jettisoning equipment that would weigh you down. When I posed this question to our recruits during our pool day, they responded with ditch "Gun Belt" "Boots" "Body armor" "Jackets". All at first blush, quite logical and reasonable but in reality…DEADLY WRONG.

I then do the demo where I stand on the edge of the pool in full uniform. Duty belt (defunct gun, rebar for magazines, keepers, rusty baton, rusty handcuffs, body armor under duty shirt, duty 511 tac boots, and a fleece/nylon jacket. Then I say my goodbyes in case it fails (joke) then fall backwards into the pool. Without ANY effort or active hands or feet, I quickly rise up to the surface and float peacefully on my back. I then pitch forward and paddle to the edge, climb out, and explain what just happened.

Over 100 LODD's over the last 60+ years are attributed to drowning. In a case close to home (lake country), an officer fell overboard while operating a RIB. He sadly drowned.

His body was located several days later by the Navy using side-scanning sonar. Upon inspection of his duty belt, it was noted that 3 of the 4 keepers were missing. This indicated forensically that he was actively trying to remove his duty belt and ran into serious trouble.

The problem with that, was that his hands were apparently occupied with trying to ditch kit instead of sculling or dog paddling to keep the head (mouth and nose) above water for basic survival. Also, when the hands dive down to the belt the body becomes more erect like a pencil dive in reverse, then changes into a sitting position and slips below the surface particularly if confusion and panic set in.

Here's the science: When I first fall into the water, every molecule of air that is trapped in ALL of the layers of clothing (from socks to t-shirt to jacket) rise upwards. However, it is all trapped within the fibers of said clothing so it literally acts like a giant airbag. It overrides all the extra weight of the gun, mags, baton etc. After some time, it will be replaced with H2O molecules (super saturation) but generally there's enough time to paddle, float, swim to safety or fight if it was a suspect who tackled you into the drink.

I then climb out and take the jacket off and toss it into the pool. It still floats on top of the water for the duration of the class. Boots taken off, guess what, remain floating. Body armor (which is heat-sealed)…floats, OC canister…same thing. The less clothing I have on, the more I tend to sink. Weird! Very counterintuitive.

Keeping the duty belt on, also allows you to fight if you need to. Radios often work for many minutes too after being immersed. Firearms still work underwater but have a few limitations due to friction affecting the bullet's range/trajectory and friction affecting normal ejection of casings which may cause malfunctions (stove pipes) etc. A few good websites out there but more should be done.

For best results, a PFD should be worn while working around the water. It limits mobility if fighting but really increases survival particularly if semi or unconsciousness occurs.

p.s. Don't try to swim against a rip tide/current (extremely fatiguing). Float and wait for help or swim angularly out of it and then to shore.

24 Light tactics

There are good times to use flashlights and not so good. Here's a couple of examples of good:

We run a sim where 2 recruits are entering a nightclub lineup to do a general walk through (Licensed Premise Check). The scenario setting is that a girl in the lineup has been assaulted and the suspect grabbed her cellphone (robbery) and fled out onto the street with a very short time delay. The other patrons are all telling the police to help her and tell the officers that "Some dude just punched her in the face and took her phone, like 30 seconds ago!" The disco lights and club soundtrack add to the initial confusion (audio stimulation and low light environment).

As the officers move up to the source (victim) she is holding her forehead with stage blood indicating a contusion/open wound. They begin asking her what happened and canvassing the crowd (which are all assisting and non-confrontational). At that point I almost ALWAYS have to yell (due to the thumping tunes) into the recruit's ears and say, "Get your flashlights out and find out what happened".

The scenario ends after they obtain a description (from

witnesses and the victim (albeit she doesn't remember much after having her bell rung), broadcast it to area units, call for EHS/EMS and exit the club out the back door and find the suspect who quickly tosses the phone behind a dumpster (on the floor).

In the debrief after they describe what they saw/heard, what they did and why they did it, I remind them of the power of light! It allows the eyes to see more and therefore process information more accurately and efficiently. It also allows cover officers to find them easier if they need help. Police tactical lights bouncing off the walls and floor is recognizable to cover and they can be of help faster instead of confusion over disco/club/dance lights that are flooding the room in a full capacity party place.

#25 More light tactics

Lights (like being trapped in a police car) can be bullet magnets.

When searching a dark environment consider using darkness as concealment from the suspect instead of lighting your position up right away. Suspects that see a light, now have a general idea of where you are so they could start shooting. To confuse them and have a tactical advantage, try lighting the area with short bursts and varying origin heights.

Changing the pattern doesn't allow them to predict your movement as easily. Also, holding it far away and up may draw them to conclude that you are directly behind the light and start shooting "up and over there" instead of right at you.

Having 2 lights is very good because you could place one on the back of the car (hallway floor) or other surface and move under the cover of light/dark to a different/better place. If they pop out and engage at the trick light, their muzzle flash with be the beacon to engage with. This all buys you time. ¼ seconds count in gun fights.

When searching and you locate a suspect, dominate with light. That means fire all those lumens into the face. It should cause the head to turn, maybe hands to come up to shield which allows you to see hands, face, hands and make a good assessment of the suspect's behavior.

We used to put captions on PowerPoint slides to give the officers some solidifying memory of the objective (Low Light Tactics…"When you find 'em, blind 'em!"). Our police oversight body read this during an education day and told me they found it to be too aggressive, malicious, and hurtful to blind somebody. After a brief discussion I explained the context and they saw it more clearly… It stayed in the lesson plan! They were illuminated and they saw the light!

#26 Cuffs On, Knees Off

For 15 years this has been a mantra in our training. Pressing humans to the floor is important to control movement. However, once the cuffs are applied, it's rare that continued body weight needs be utilized even if the subject is still struggling.

If the handcuffed suspect is in a prone position (face down) simply holding onto each elbow in a C-clamp style on the elbows/upper arm restricts their attempt to get up or turn and kick, bite, etc. You can also press down or staple their hips to the ground until a hobble restraint device (or similar tool) can be applied to the ankles.

The C-clamp allows the bellows effect of their lungs to operate better than with body weight laying on their back/torso.

Sometimes if there is continued body weight applied when cuffed, they may appear to still be fighting. However, that behavior may actually indicate that they are running out of breath and are panicking and potentially fighting for their life. That (if the officers aren't trained to recognize the difference) can be mis-interpreted as continued violence and fighting for escape. It's a fine line, but also, it's a fine mess if they can't breathe.

Recognize the difference. Also, if someone is in the throes

of Excited Delirium, EMS needs to attend priority and depending on the assessment, may need to chemically restrain the subject and get the subject to ER ASAP. *See tip # 27 Excited Delirium…like as in the next page!

#27 Excited Delirium

In a nutshell Excited Delirium is categorized as a medical emergency. However, medical assistance in almost ALL cases cannot be administered until the subject is restrained. It is too dangerous for paramedics to deal safely if a subject is extremely aggressive and thrashing about etc.

What it looks like? Any bizarre, irrational, non-communicative, violent, naked, sweaty, (or totally dry), freaked out looking people that don't seem to feel pain, are very strong (no matter what their body shape), are smashing windows (affliction with glass) or running around through traffic etc.

What causes it? Stress, drugs, booze, mental health, no sleep, cocaine, less cocaine, more cocaine, no cocaine, stomped cocaine, meth, more meth, hallucinations, less meth etc. and/or pre-existing medical or psychological conditions.

What can you do to help? Call for ambulance and other units. Tell neighbors to go inside and lock the doors and stay away from windows. Slow the police commands down and try not to make sudden or jerky movements. Keep the convo to calming tones and re-assurance that the FBI or CIA isn't coming anymore (if they are having paranoid delusions). "Radio them" and tell them to stay away.

Tell the subject, even if they can't talk except for making

animal grunts (keening) that help is coming. Turn down super flashy lights but still have some on to be found easier by cover cars and EMS. Contain. Then when timely, Restrain. Straight to ER.

The EMS will hopefully have license to administer benzodiazepine and/or other drugs (chemical restraints) to mitigate fatal symptoms/outcomes. Try to find out from friends/street folk/ what they have taken and any name that might shine light on other medical complications that may have been noted on a prior report.

And finally, make copious amounts of notes. A coroner who we had a very candid conversation with regarding our Ex-D Lesson Plan teaching points stated, "Any officer that attends one of these calls is holding a stick that is brown on both ends". That is due to the likelihood of having to use force to restrain (which has shown to be extremely difficult) which therefore can also appear egregious and excessive. It is also due to the fact that the subject is in significant medical distress. This event may have been brewing for days and culminated when police were called to help. If the subject passes away proximal to police contact, an in-custody death investigation takes place. Both situations are tragic for *everybody* including the subject's family.

#28 You don't have any guns or knives in the car, do you?

Kind of like tip # 3 (remember...hand grenades?) but a bit different. Here's why:

I was watching a really good Netflix documentary called Dope. Real people, real drugs, real gangs, real cops, comforting to see we are all facing the same problems...but maybe not so intense at times! There was one of many vehicle stops conducted during the interdiction and interruption of runners/dealers near the Detroit Toronto border.

The officer approached the driver and explained the reason for the stop but then said, "You don't have any guns or knives in the car do you?"

That question is way too easy to answer cause he's already prompted the negative reply for an easy..."No".

It's simple for people to lie when presented with a glaring negative theme. A better form to pose the question is clearly "Keep your hands in plain sight sir/ma'am. Thanks. Now, are there any guns or knives or other weapons in this car, or on your person?"

Then watch the face and hands. Kind of like a Texas (Detroit, L.A. Boston, Toronto etc.) hold'em. Most human beings under psychological stress will show some indicators.

Look for things like looking away from you when they answer. Lying to the dashboard or passenger is easier than to another human being. *

Responding back with "What?" or "Sorry, what was that?" when they clearly heard you without interference of ambient noise (music, traffic, passengers talking etc.) is a forced way of buying more time to come up with a non-inculpatory response.

Not responding at all, or a…pause…may indicate a nervous over-ride of the frontal cortex (reasoning brain) trying to come up with an answer while holding a shit hand.

You can always dilute the stress by saying "It's not a big deal if there is, but it is a big deal if your reach for it. So, let's get through this safely now". "We are not here to hurt you" (sound familiar?)! What great audio/video evidence if it did turn into an OIS seconds or minutes later.

*Some cultures will look away while answering a person in authority such as an elder, so know your communication traits and customs of everybody you serve and/or arrest!

#29 "Tap Rack Ready" after a gun grab

Gun grabs are showing up more and more during arrests. Desperate suspects, motivated to avoid arrest or just murderous intent. Sometimes suspects try to disarm officers to kill themselves or someone else. Either way this is not a theft. It is an attempted murder. We have to be prepared for such an attack.

Some gun grabs occur when the gun is out of the holster and in close proximity to the suspect. Sometimes it is a surprise ambush and the suspect grabs the exposed grip of the pistol or scrambles during an arrest to pull the gun out by attacking the thumb releases, snaps or locking mechanisms.

Keeping the holstered gun in the holster is paramount but also fighting back fast and switching the predator prey relationship by causing massive injuries (psychological or physical or both) is vital. Violently attacking the trachea, side of neck or base of skull (soft fleshy part) usually results in trauma that can cause the person to become non-functional (at least for a moment) as their primal survival systems overrides the input.

Once clear, it is a good idea to tap rack ready as the magazine release button may have inadvertently been pressed causing a failure to fire due to an unseated mag. Make distance, scan breathe, call for resources. Do a wet check and let the dust and other airborne particulates settle if you were injured or rounds were fired. Practice shooting from unconventional platforms such as: Suspect on top, suspect on bottom, suspect on side, suspect straddling etc. (Be wary of touching muzzle to suspect if/when shooting them). So, guess what, see next tip!

#30 Contact Shots…not really

If during the above-noted, or other close quarter deadly force battle, you decide to shoot, give the pistol room to work.

In the "old days" it was called a contact shot where the muzzle was placed against the suspect to deliver a controlled shot to a viable target. Problem being is that terminology has stuck around, and is still used in many firearms and UOF training descriptions. Problem also being that some of us (me included) carried revolvers! Dating myself I know (as in era not like dating dating). You could successfully fire a round (or 2 or more) with the muzzle slammed up against a body.

However, if you press a semi-auto hard against a body part there is a chance that the muzzle will ever so slightly be pushed out of battery causing a failure to fire. So, "In a pinch, give it an in inch" (yup that's mine)!

There are some great innovators out there in the field that have experimented with unconventional grips on guns combined when deadly force CQB is the environment.

For example, Don Gulla and his team discovered and documented a super powerful way to grip the pistol (normal grip) and also a firm overhand grip (with the other hand) on the barrel/sliderail etc. and successfully deliver a round with concentric pressure which keeps the pistol in battery!

This is a very strong position if body to body and the suspect is also grabbing hands/arms/gun etc. The officer's hand will not be damaged by the slide rails/ejection port action and all he or she needs to do is manually rack to chamber the next round. This can be repeated as often as necessary until the threat of the disarm (attempted murder/suicide or both) in neutralized.

#31 Verbally Searching a Suspect

Searching is one of the most important tasks an officer has to perform. Many officers, jailers and prisoners have been injured or killed by missed weapons during searches. Suspects can be quite tricky in hiding weapons or officers can be rushing a search. So… take your time!

The golden rule of searching is simply: Handcuff First, Search Second.

The danger of "frisking" or "patting down" somewhat lies in the terminology. Frisk sounds hurried and fast, and pat down insinuates not thorough.

A good first step (after the legal requirements are met) is to build a rapport with the subject. That means explaining to them the process. "Hey bud, I'm gonna search you now. Don't move around while we do this ok?"

A good question to ask right off the hop is: "Is this your jacket?"

If you provide the suspect with this "out" and they are in possession of contraband/drugs/stolen property or weapons they may reply with "Ah, no, I found it in the dumpster" or "It's my friend's, I borrowed it" or "It was at our table in the night club, it looked like mine in the dark".

Well, all those could be true, but it is also a possible

indication that they don't want to be caught with it and bear the consequences. Other evidence if needed (Video-CCTV) witness statements etc. can corroborate or counter their claims.

Giving them that alternative theme may take some stress out and keep them calm as they may think that the ramifications won't be so dire if something is found.

Just like Tip # 28 about asking drivers or occupants of a vehicle about possession or able access to weapons, the same model can be used for non-vehicle environments:

"Do you have any weapons on you?" pause…

That pause should be used to study the verbal and more importantly, their Body Language.

Although the more studied science of human deception requires a baseline of conversation and observations of non-threatening communication before the hot question is asked, a couple of things can be listened for or seen:

A common deceptive response is repeating the question back to you so they can buy some stall time for a strategy of deceit.

Officer: "Sir, are there any weapons on you or in the car?"

Them: "Are there any weapons in the car?" (with an

increasing high rising voice tone on the subject word "weapons").

Or in other investigative questions:

Officer: "What's your date of birth?"

Them: "What's my birthdate?"

Or:

Officer : "Were you just in the 7-11 a couple of minute ago?"

Them: "Seven-eleven?" phonetically SE-ven e-LEV-en?" "Roller coastering" of tone may be indicating stress as with the attempted "middling" of the tone back to "normal" levels.

Interesting note. Several thousand years ago the Chinese had a way of determining if a person was lying. They filled the suspect's mouth with dry rice. He then was told to spit it out. If it was still dry, they ruled he was likely lying. Anxiousness in humans decreases blood flow to the digestive system and in turn the salivary glands limit production. (Don't really need to eat during a threat!). This "dry mouth" rice was then seen to be telling. I would submit rather, that having a person in authority forcing uncooked rice into my face would make me anxious but who wanted to argue back then?!

People sometimes also have a drier esophagus and tend to

swallow awkwardly under stress. Gulp! Court defensible? Doubt it, but this may allow you to continue asking and verify your intuitions and look for other tells which could enhance your safety which of course is a decent priority. Again, what is important when looking for and detecting deceit is to have a baseline of behaviors to measure truthfulness against. Synchrony is helpful too. That is: Are the answers matching up with the body language in time? If a person is asked a question and is truthful that the answer is "No", they will generally begin to first shake their head left and right while saying "No". If they answer "No" *then* shake their head a moment or two afterwards it may indicate that they are trying to catch up with their lie. Prey animals will often freeze to avoid being detected by predators. If a person is "frozen" it is most likely subconscious that they just want to hide from the threat and hope it goes somewhere else! Hard to prove in court but could prove effective in yours and other's safety.

#32 "We'll find you a fight kid"

When a class of police recruits return from their Block 2 (actual road deployment 4 months with an FTO) we have a gym fireside chat about things they experienced relating to use of force and if any of the tactics we taught were used and if so, how did it go?

We get common themes usually about dealing with mental health subjects, some knife, some gun, foot pursuits, lots of control on the ground etc.

On a couple of occasions, it was learned that some of their squad mates (hopefully NOT the field trainer) would say things like "O.K. kid, tonight we will find you a fight!" Kind of like a rite of passage or must do to be part of the team. It is quite possibly one of the most dangerous things to suggest to a recruit (or any officer).

Why?

Well, what if the officer is really good at reading body language, excellent as using their verbal skills to de-escalate, fit, competent and strong but for some reason feels that they have to now get into something to appease the boneheads that suggested it?

Along comes a call (go figure) and the officer uses force which causes the subject to fall to the ground, but they unfortunately strike their head casing a brain bleed and near death result. Can you imagine what the defense actually…prosecutor, would do if the earlier insinuation bore its ugly head? Let's play civil litigation lawyer just for fun…and of course the almighty cash.

"Ladies and Gentlemen of this fine jury, as you learned, the witnesses in the coffee shop overheard the group of officers saying O.K. kid, tonight we will find you a fight. Obviously my client was targeted and was a victim of a pre-planned attack. The fall injury from the hard ground may have been unintentional as the expert evidence showed, but the pure malice and egregious forethought of conflict is what really is on trial here".

"I put it to the court that if not pre-determined, then at the very least, conducted in such a malicious way as to prove intent to injure. We are asking for $14,000,000,000,000,000 settlement for loss of future earnings including punitive damages blah blah blah etc etc etc". I rest my case!

Also, the stress of all the investigations and cop v. cop has no price for all the problems that was caused by tempting bravado. My tip: Never Start Fights…Only Finish Them!

#33 333

An exhaustive search was conducted on my agency's police involved shootings over about a 25-year period. Some interesting and important characteristics were found. This evidenced-based research helped us to craft training and qualifications that were more conducive to what the officers may encounter on the streets. A common theme was discovered in that the numbers 3-3-3 kept coming up. That is:

3 Rounds

3 Meters (yards)

3 Seconds

The average number of rounds fired was 3.

The encounter took place within 3 meters (yards).

The duration of the actual engagement was 3 seconds.

What does this tell us?

That a fair amount of deadly force encounters happen spontaneously in and around vehicles, persons checks, doorways, spontaneous knife attacks, gun out grabs etc. Not a lot of long-sighted shots. Most were "Oh shit" moments where the suspect attacked first (police are behind the curve by virtue of their job as it relates to Action vs. Reaction). A lot of one-handed shots, non-sighted, draw point and shoot situations.

There were some outside the curve (25 meters plus) and also super close quarter (ground) and some one-shot wonders and 10 round shoots. Our scenarios and qualifications adjusted to this research and are therefore more akin to what members will possibly encounter. Train like you fight… (not my saying).

#34 Physically searching a suspect

Golden Rule carryover…Handcuff first, Search second

If you are searching for weapons, give yourself the best chance of finding them.

Quite often, officers don't have a set pattern that they follow. Today I'll start with the left side waistband, then left leg, then right shoe/sock, left arm etc. Tomorrow, I'll do back then front then top or wait…bottom. A consistent pattern or "habit method" is better.

For example, for a standing (or actually all positioned) subject it is best to start with the areas they still have access to (even in cuffs) such as the rear waistband/pockets.

Then proceed methodically around to the front waistband and then front pockets, proceeding back around to the rear and double check making sure nothing was missed, then begin the consistent pattern whatever yours is.

A Ven diagram is overlapping circles. Visualize the overlapping circles being the waistband. If you hit it twice or three times that's a good thing. Most weapons are carried where the suspect can access them during a conflict. Sleeves are also good places to conceal knives as they are generally flat and are sometimes missed due to the shape of the forearm being similarly flat in design.

Socks offer support for knives. Ankle holsters occasionally are worn. Although, a lot of criminals don't like to have a fixed holster because if they ditch the gun, the holster will be found, raising suspicions and grounds, and also potentially matching a nearby found firearm.

General rule: If you find an empty holster, look within a several yard radius of the subject. It may be in a trash can, under a car or in a bush etc. which they stashed it in upon seeing you roll up but not so far away that someone else gets it. Guns are money!

Back to searching:

It is better to Press and Assess as opposed to patting which looks like "putting out small fires". Slapping/patting doesn't give the brain long enough to interpret what the hand is "telling" it.

Pressing and assessing will alert you to something that feels untoward: bulky/metallic (weapon) soft pliable (bag of drugs) etc. Like pretty much everything else, take your time. Sliding your hand up and down limbs runs the risk of getting poked by a needle or cut by a blade like sliding your hand up and down a 2x4. Wood that make sense? (Sorry, dad joke). Press and Assess is best.

When you find one weapon, look for the next and so on until you are satisfied that it's done. You may be so pumped that you found the murder weapon that you neglect to find something else.

Handcuff locking mechanisms haven't changed for decades as with handcuff keys. Due to their small size, cuff keys can be hidden in several places: Waistbands; taped to inside of belts; socks; sleeves; inside heel of shoes are all common areas because they can still access if cuffed and motivated. Sweatbands, brims of ball hats etc. provide stashes for keys too. Some hardcore criminals place plastic keys in their mouth.

Jewelry has been fashioned (pardon the pun) to have the key part included. An officer was killed after the suspect accessed a cuff key/shim from a dangling necklace which ultimately aided in his escape and subsequent attack upon arrival at the jail sally port.

Desperation breeds ingenuity.

Modified keys are also available online and in some tactical survival outfitters that can attach to shoelace ends, hoodie strings and anything else imaginable. Make great stocking stuffers for the good guys in case of an officer hostage situation. Long shot, but comforting to have in a pinch. Kind of like a TK.

I arrested a drug dealer one block away from the police station. I had observed him putting out and hiding money and drugs in his socks/shoe. After he was cuffed, I took his shoes off and recovered the crack and cash. He also has a Canada-Wide immigration warrant. I walked him over to cells. Not long after, I got a call from the jail sergeant who asked me to come up. I thought he was going to say "Nice work good job on the warrant and dope". Nope! I had missed a weapon. UNDER the dealer's shoe insole was an awl (a very sharp pointed metal "blade" with a wooden handle). Crafty bugger had crafted out a channel where it was hidden. From that point forward I always removed the stinky insoles. Never found another one but never forgot that one.

#35 Jits, Judo, Karate, Boxing, Muay Thai, etc.

A lot has been discussed over the years about which martial arts are best for police training. Simple answer is not so simple!

The complexities of different martial arts are complex in nature. Nice stall! So many rules apply, and the many intricate techniques are generally time-honored and passed down from Grand Masters to the white belts which happens in dojos/clubs all over the world.

The problem with focusing on one style is that it limits the LE student with confines during actual combat. For example, in a Jiu-jitsu (spelling varies around the globe) club, it is prohibited for the players to strike as it would be dangerous for the students to hammer fist each other in the neck or intentionally target the groin. In Karate or Judo, one would likely be ejected from the Association if they knowingly dropped a knee to the back of the head of their opponent after a takedown. In wrestling, no kicks or punches are allowed and so on and so on.

It is important to understand the diametrically opposed functions of playing a sport versus protecting yourself or somebody else in a real-world violent situation.

Absolutely, knowledge and skills are, and must be, gleaned from various arts so that the officer can have the best chance at winning a street encounter. Therefore, it is kind of a blend.

Judo for upsetting balance and making people fall against their will. Striking arts to allow the officer to be able to hit when required to cause a motor dysfunction, pain, distraction, or in high levels, unconsciousness etc.

Jits and wrestling to be able to maintain control of someone while on the ground and also get out from underneath somebody (trap 'n roll, bridge, shrimp, sweep) etc.

Krav Maga is a very free style of self-defense and seems to capture a lot of principles of striking, eye rakes/gouges and ferocity. Some in the police circle find it too aggressive without the requisite duty of care for a suspect. It's a beauty for the public to learn to garner situational awareness and counter-tactics to attacks and also good for violent LE encounters.

Martial arts are a great vehicle to encourage fitness, respect of others, discipline, and many other benefits for police/corrections/security and personal growth. The problem is it generally takes years and years and a lifetime of dedication to be proficient in EACH or ALL of them. Cops sometimes don't have time and unfortunately some are straightforward lazy. Sorry. Truth hurts sometimes. Whatever the borrowed skill sets are, they must be easy to learn and easy to perform under stress while meeting criteria for duty of care and reasonableness. Bread and Butter stuff as they say.

We try to semantically rebrand systems to meet the needs. Perhaps "LEDO" The Law Enforcement Way may be catchy? Yes, that's mine but go ahead and start a movement club!! Just give me honorary status and a free black and blue Gi. Thx!

This might wrap up (Ha Ha control tactics pun) our goal as police officers: "Be extremely courteous to ALL people, except during a fight, then after you win, be extremely courteous again".

Train Well to avoid the Train Wreck. (yup)!

#36 Give the injured officer work to do

Officers that have been shot or stabbed or otherwise seriously injured will likely be in a state of shock due to the massive dump of adrenaline and other survival hormones that helped them during the fight or to protect from pain/injury. While you are carrying them to a rescue location for EMS, keep their mind occupied with conversation other than natural "hang in there" dialogue.

The mind is their most powerful asset, so keep them involved with the event. Tell them "We got you brother/sister" (family is powerful) and then begin asking fact finding questions if needed to capture the suspect(s).

"What was the license plate of the car?" as opposed to "Do you remember the plate?"

"Tell me what he looked like" as opposed to "Did you see what he looked like?"

"How many were there?" as opposed to "Was there more than one?"

They still want to help so after the necessary description and direction of travel is obtained, give them a job.

"Jerry, hold my flashlight and light up the alley so I can see better"

"The tourniquet is on, so the bleeding is stopped. Now which way did he run?"

Sitting or maybe laying an injured officer down is better than them standing propped up against a building or car. If they do happen to lose consciousness it will mitigate a secondary or tertiary injury from a fall. Laying down also allows for homeostasis to occur, keeping the blood in the core and also facilitating oxygenated blood in getting to the brain to stay conscious. Raise the injured limb above the pump (heart) to use gravity in their favor.

Some officers will tell you to tell their family that they love them. Respond with "You tell them that when we get to the hospital"

Winning Mind is all about the Mind Winning. So let's stack the odds in their favor with YES YES YES.

#37 Give the self-injured suicidal person work to do

One of our scenarios involves an officer who is told by a citizen, and also a bus driver, that a guy was sitting on the bus bench and was crying, didn't get on the bus, and mentioned "his life was over". No mention of weapons.

The officer attends to the bus stop in question and sees a role player sitting on the bench overtly crying with hands covering his face. After the officer advises dispatch that he will be out with a despondent person at the location, the role payer slowly produces a knife and begins to cut his wrist (theatrical blood in slice lines to represent cutting).

The scenario is designed to have the officer make distance, update radio of the knife, and mitigate risk to other passerbyers (it's now a word!). He then takes out his firearm and keeps it in Suel or low ready in case the subject turns from suicidal to homicidal and gets up and closes the distance. The officer moves to a better place (shielding/cover). *It's perfectly o.k. to talk to people with a gun in hand(s).

The officer then identifies himself as the police and commands him to put the knife down.

The RP doesn't. The officer then engages in de-escalation dialogue saying things like:

Officer: "We're not here to hurt you"

Subject: "Go away. Leave me alone"

Officer: "What's your name?"

Subject: "John"

Officer: "O.K. John, my name is Wayne"

John: "Why the fuck do you care anyway?"

Officer: "Cause I care about the people in my neighborhood and I want to help you. It's what I do"

Officer: "What's making you feel this way?"

John: "My girlfriend left me, it's not worth fucking living anymore"

Officer "Your girlfriend left you. That is super difficult man. I hear you"

Officer: "Hey John, I'm gonna help you but it's safer if you drop the knife ok?"

John: "No. Stay the fuck away from me"

Officer: "O.K. I will. No problem. You got it"

   That conversation in its natural state took approximately 45 seconds. This is what I like to call the Tick Talk Tactic.

The Tick is time. As in, the longer you can keep talking to

someone and have them keep talking to you, the more time is created for resources to attend the scene: Cover, Less Lethal, K9, EMS, Traffic/Motor Units, Transit Authority to assist with potential re-routes if the event becomes protracted etc.

The Talk is non-threatening or non-blamatory (another new word) and should be focused on de-escalation and crisis intervention. Listening, Empathy, Asking and Paraphrasing (Dr. George Thompson's <u>Verbal Judo</u>™ LEAPS. A must read for LEO's).

Back to the scene:

John starts whimpering and body crying and drops the knife by his feet.

Officer: "Thanks John. The ambulance is coming real soon. What I need you to do now is hold the cut on your wrist with your other hand and now raise it above your head. It will help slow the bleeding down, ok?"

John: "O.K. I don't want to die."

Officer: "It's o.k. you won't die."

Here's the job part: "Just keep the pressure on it. You're doing great bud, nice work".

There could be a Taser option too if necessary but that will depend usually on a partner present with lethal overwatch incase the subject changes his behavior and begins to be posture aggressively.

The great thing about Tick Talk is that it buys time. Time to bring resources. The type of self-harm may also dictate tactics.

****Never compromise officer safety with CID (Crisis Intervention & De-escalation). If it works that's a win. If it doesn't, you know, and so does the oversight body (if you have those) that you tried your best to help the person who ultimately is driving the call. We just try to steer people back on track. Sometimes the media and public think that all an officer needs to do is use "de-escalation" and nothing bad will ever happen. They obviously have never worn our boots. Try your best, but don't risk the rest. Yup…mine! Sorry but I love inventing catchy phrases! Should have maybe been in advertising. Just Do It…nah, that would never work.

*Just recently listened to Lt. Jim Glennon at the ILEETA Conference in St. Louis.. He is a consummate professional and a true LEADER. His style and mentality should be in ALL agencies and Police Academies. One great takeaway was when he so eloquently stated that "De-escalation isn't a tactic, it is a goal."

#38 Let your toes do the walking

We just had another recruit class (64 officers) come through the doors. Day 1 of Officer Safety Training covers fundamentals. We cover off the numeric relative positions when interacting with a subject.

1. Directly in front
1.5 Field interview (slightly off to the side)
2. Directly Beside
2.5 45-degree angle from the rear
3. Directly behind

After discussing pros and cons of each, we call out a number and they move to it. On average when we call a number that requires them to travel a fair bit around the clock, about 50% walk backwards with their heels leading the way.

We then ask them what the risks with walking backwards are. They correctly say bumping into things and/or falling. On the gym mats there are minimal vertical changes or tripping hazards. But out on the road they may trip over curbs, rocks, uneven terrain, people, traffic, telephone poles, stairs etc. etc.

The toes, even in shoes, are designed to adapt to hazards as they are flexible and very effective sensory indicators in sending signals to the brain about the environment regarding terrain.

This information is a steppingstone (sorry) to more dynamic movement such as knife attacks, multiple assailants and more!

Master tactics are the basics mastered. (Not mine but great)!

#39 What's the problem with "What's the problem?"

In the early 1990's (yup, old guy) there was great push for police agencies to become pro-active in solving community issues. There was lots of concern from administrators and city officials that all cops do is drive around in squad cars (as opposed to walking the beat and foot patrolling their neighborhoods) and respond reactively to calls of service.

So was born Problem Oriented Policing. It had a catchy phrase. Senior officers and managers broke out into think tanks retreats, kibitzing with like-minded officials that all read books on broken windows and crime reduction strategies, including all paid trips to retreats and conferences. Fantastic (if you were the ones on the vacay)!

Actually, it was not a bad initiative but like everything else was a new and different mandate. And as we know, cops can't stand two things: 1. Change, and 2. The way things are!

So then came training classrooms filled with patrol officers before shift, and sometimes replaced use of force days, with the new game in town titled <u>Problem Oriented Policing</u>. Just saying, there were a lot of instant promotions going on at the time and the horse was well out of the gate with dozens of riders jockeying for position! Not my bag baby!

However, what the main goal was, was for the officers to connect with their citizens (awesome) and gather intel on crime and disorder issues (awesome) and come up with solutions as a group (awesome). Something we actually did pretty good on our own anyways, or so I thought. (Maybe I thought we were good at catching bad guys…actually we were no doubt). Anyways, the programs played out and it helped in different ways. Done.

The side issue problem (of which I titled this tip) with POP was that we then started to hear police on first contact with people say, "What's the problem?". Well, that's a problem because it creates a lot of issues when people are reminded there is one. Sematic yes, unrealistic no.

Often officers would then hear "Well, you guys are the problem. I called 6 times about the crack house next door in the last week, and nothing got done. Now, our house got broken into and we just lost all our fuckin' stuff."

At a domestic, same thing. "Well, you guys are the problem. He got arrested last night and now he comes home and beats the shit out of me" etc.

So, long diatribe short, a better introduction as you roll up to the call is "How can we help you?"

Wow, what a concept! Someone calls 911 and they get help!

It also elicits their solutions and acts as a collaboration tool. People (for the most part) like to get help when they can't solve things themselves. They will feel comforted by your offer and will often calm down when asked that simple human act of compassion and assistance.

Side note: Actually, Bottom Note

Sometimes, officers are pasted in the public or some media as all being bad. Some actually are, or are more likely, poorly selected and/or poorly trained. The unfortunate thing is that the good cops get "discriminated professionally" and have a hard time dealing with that, and struggle with motivation to do their job after being labelled. Here's a simple math equation and a solve for that problem.

1 officer who treats people poorly on a regular basis can mathematically bring down a department's reputation: 10 negative contacts a shift. The recipient tells their negative story to 10 people. That's 100 a day. Times 4 shifts per week times 48 weeks a year, times 10 years equals 192,000 negative impressions. WOW! So, let's do this: Continue to be Uber courteous. Holding doors open for people, thank people for their cooperation. Smile. Wave. Lots of you do this already. Keep it up! Don't lose faith. THIS is the way to win back the hearts and minds of the public: 100 cops who treat 10 people super good, times 5 (bad experiences are shared twice as much as good) times 4 weeks, times…well, you get the math!

*Thanks Dr. George Thompson

#40 Officer Involved Shooting…get some sleep cycles

When an officer is involved in a critical incident, they need some time to process the event before writing it down in a formal statement or providing the Major Crime investigators a full statement. This is because if they provide detailed information immediately following the shooting, it will quite likely be inaccurate! Why? Several reasons.

It is common for the stress of the situation to elevate heart rates over 200 BPM. Massive dumps of adrenaline and other survival hormones are released during such an event. It sometimes takes several days for the system to re-calibrate and balance out. Memories can be altered or clouded, and things such as distances, descriptions, time and other important facts can be way out from the actual parameters.

Most studied doctors and police psychologists suggest 2-3 sleep cycles before a detailed statement should be given. Also, there is the possibility that the officer was physically injured which adds to the body and mind's need to recover.

On the scene information must be given if necessary to the other officers in case there is an outstanding suspect, vehicle description or other important information to share. Police unions and legal teams are now well aware of the effects of an OIS. Automatic legal representation is often a done deal in most switched-on agencies. The use of force world can be highly litigious. Be a winner in ALL arenas. Look after yourself.

#41 How many rounds did you or your partner fire, what exactly was the suspect wearing at the time and other insignificant questions in a life and death match, and other beauties of educating non-police people.

There are many police oversight bodies in place in cities and counties around North America (and the rest of the world). We invited "ours" out to the Tactical Training Center to participate in an officer safety mini training session to see how police are trained. They were to act as the officers.

The day started off in the classroom with a PowerPoint and frank discussion about statistics and police interactions highlighting the over 1,000,000 police contacts with less that 1% ending in a use of force event. Then showing that even less than that resulted in a less lethal application, and obviously an even lower percentage resulting in a police involved shooting.

Hollywood, of course, would rarely sell a movie with the reality of police interactions. BORING (for those that enjoy violence). FANTASTIC for those that are peace officers (but still kinda boring nonetheless).

We then showed them videos of real violence and victims getting stabbed and store owners getting shot for a 26 ounce bottle of booze and a carton of darts. Pure asocial predators that prey on the public without concern for others. Yes, they are out there.

We then took them into the gym and demonstrated a variety of training drills emphasizing reaction time, adapting to low light environments, the challenges of physical control, de-escalation dialogue tactics, Tasers, OC etc. We address the question about "Why don't cops shoot knives out of hands or wound people in the leg?". We also did this "exposure training" with a dozen members of the media on a "Media Training Day".

We then asked for volunteers to participate in sims to put themselves in the officer's shoes.

In one scenario we used a role player of ours who weighs about 115lbs. Two volunteers were simply asked to control her and place her hands behind her back in preparation for cuffing because she was causing a disturbance and running around the neighborhood yelling at everyone to fight her. They were not able to. The RP was simply holding a prone turtle position.

We then asked the "officers" what they would feel like if she had started punching, kicking, biting, and spitting. They really didn't know what to do or even say. Bit of an eye opener for a "simple" 2 v 1 interaction.

We explained the tactics required to overcome that type of resistance and that it's not just muscular strength but more about teamwork and understanding the principles of controlling movement, all the while ensuring nothing unintended happens.

We then simply added in "Oh, by the way, while you were on the ground focusing all your energy and attention on her, the boyfriend/girlfriend came around the corner of the house with a 2x4 and brained your partner with it. Now what?" They got quiet and started to pay more attention.

We then did our classic demo where we had a trainer (JR) play a suspect armed with a pistol (sim gun loaded with blank training cartridges) tucked in his waistband. I tell the group that I had just walked back to my patrol car when this guy walks around the corner of the strip mall after a holdup which simultaneously gets broadcast. Right time at the right place (for the police that is. His is the opposite).

Without a chance to move unseen to shielding/cover/concealment, I ask the crowd what to do.

Several blurt out "Take out your gun!"

Awesome. I do. Finger on frame pointing at buddy.

"Then what?" I ask.

"Tell him to Freeze!"

Coolish. I Say "Police Don't Move. I see the gun. Now put

your hands in the air. If you reach for it you will be shot. Do you understand?"

"Call for back-up" they shriek.

So I get on the air and tell radio I have a suspect at gunpoint who has a weapon in his waistband likely associated the robbery call.

We "freeze" in time. I ask the almighty loaded (pardon the pun) question:

"If he grabs his gun, who is gonna win?"

"You will!" they respond in chorus.

I say, "Is it important for the public that I win?"

"Yes, so that he doesn't shoot any innocent people"

"Am I innocent?" (Deep philosophical debate and laughter ensues)!

Now back to the drill:

I then tell Johnny out loud "When you decide, you shoot at me"

The crowd is hushed. He looks furtively beside him, sniffs nervously and goes for it. I respond with finger to trigger, and we blast away. At best it is a tie.

After the dust settles, I ask the group why it was pretty

much even. (A media person had it on her iPhone and we watched it back in slow motion. Photo Finish).

Usually someone with some sport or military experience or knowledge blurts out. "Because he is in action, and you are in reaction".

I respond with "Thank you! Recruiting office opens at 0700hrs!"

More nervous laughter.

We then have a platform to explain decision making, OODA Loops, ¾ second time frame to Assess Plan and Act and other teaching models for LE human performance. And we also inform them that the average time to fire one round from a semi-auto pistol is ¼ second (4 rounds in 1 second basically). ¼ seconds matter in a gun fight.

We then talk about other things like seeking cover, shooting on the move, never giving up, knowing how to attenuate critical hemorrhages with a TK (with one hand) etc.

Now most heads are nodding.

The second drill is a role player dressed in a hoody, that has a visible pistol showing in his waist band. The story line relates of a call members responded to on the local Skytrain rail platform: Several citizens had called 911 saying that a male was approaching passengers and threatening them with a gun.

When units arrived, they saw the suspect in a crowd. They waited for it to lessen, then challenged him with guns drawn and pointed.

I stop the story and add this:

"Now you are the officer. The suspect has both hands raised beside his head. In slow motion, the role player is going to begin lowering his right hand in increments and pausing at several points (basically every 3 inches). Knowing what you now know about reaction time, and trying not to get killed, I'm asking YOU when you would pull/press your trigger. Please indicate your deadly force decision by raising you hand up. Let's begin".

The RP then moves his hand from a right-angle elbow bend to a 45-degree palm forward position and stops. One participant's hand goes up. Some glance over at him to see who it was. He glares back at them through his eyebrows. The RP then moves it slowly another 45 degrees to palm facing floor, fingers splayed open and stops. 2 more "shooters" hands go up. He them moves his hand towards his centerline, palm facing his belly. 4 hands up.

(Half the group still not shooting).

He then shows his hand to wrap around the grip of the exposed gun. 3 more hands up. Several people raise their hands halfway in the air. I call out that "You can't half shoot someone!" Their hands embarrassingly go up, some back down!

Still not everyone commits to pulling/pressing the trigger.

The RP then inches the gun out halfway. Another hand. A couple more inches out, then all the way out and a couple more "shoot" him. He then points it directly at me then the last hands are raised. The last people were concerned that the gun might not be real. I asked them "Are you willing to get shot in the neck to then figure it out?" Some people think that the suspect has to shoot first before police are lawfully permitted to engage.

Most seem a little shaken that they had to shoot someone to protect themselves but admit they had no choice.

We then tell them what really happened that day at the train station…

As the officers were yelling commands and clearing citizens out of the way, the suspect blurted out "It's not real" and at the same time immediately reached and tossed the replica sliding it across the floor. No officers shot. They were behind the curve in such a time deficit because after we timed it, it took $60/100^{th}$ of a second for him to dump it on the ground. Lucky for him and also the semi-crowded backdrop. Suspect was charged with possession of a weapon dangerous to public peace (albeit a fake). The crowd is warming up to the realities of biomechanics during lethal force encounters.

We then break for the bathroom then move back into the classroom for a safety briefing and explanation about the upcoming scenarios. We give them a Coles notes on the value of Reality Based Training.

Two participants are partnered up and issued with training pistols charged with blank training cartridges (NLTA), inert OC spray and a training baton (one of those awesome blue ones) and eye pro. Meanwhile, back in the sim room, role players and assessors have gathered to play out a nightclub lineup turned stabbing.

The "cops" are led into the ante room, and given the following briefing:

You are on uniformed patrol and are walking the beat. As you are walking past a busy nightclub, you hear a bit of an argument over loud pre-party lineup bumpin' tunes. You tell radio that you will at the Republic for a possible disturbance.

"Begin scenario!"

We open the door, and they walk in. The padded sim room "A" is decorated with faux brick wall wallpaper, a line-up stanchion with ropes and a nightclub neon sign. The lights are dimmed to evening mode. 10 people are standing around waiting to get in but there are 2 people getting a little heated.

The "cops" stand and observe and take in the scene. A beefy bouncer stands cross-armed at the front of the lineup.

On our hand signal a role player overtly takes out a knife and repeatedly stabs one of the others in the stomach (cyclical piston like motion congruent with edged weapon thrusting attack). The victim holds his stomach, blood begins showing on his white t-shirt and the crowd begins to scream. The suspect quickly moves to the back of the line, turns and then acting surprised notices the police standing 15 feet away. He slowly moves towards them raising the knife in an overhand ice-pick posture. They both shoot him. He falls at their feet. We ask them "What's Important Now" (a great Brian Willis line). They respond with "Call an ambulance!" so we tell them to do that. Then we remind them about what to do next. We end the scenario and ask them our 3 favorite Ken Murray post sim questions:

What did you see/hear?

What did you do?

And why did you do it?

They are visibly shaken, and we give them time to bring the HR down. They relay the story pretty much how it played out. We nod along and give our take on their decisions and tactics. They go back to the classroom and the next two come in etc. *We remind them not to discuss the particulars of their shooting with their partner.

We run another sim which is a suicidal subject who is in crisis. There is no force used and they are expected to use dialogue (CID) and resources to effectively calm the person down and get them medical assistance. Nice work, good job!

Back in the classroom, we pretend to don a suit jacket and tie, an empty file folder (with an official case # printed on it) and introduce ourselves as Investigators with the Independent Investigations Office.

We separate them and begin a line of questioning.

"You were just involved in an incident at the Republic Nightclub where you shot a subject correct?"

They recount the event.

We jump right to the heart of the matter.

"How many rounds did you fire?"

They say "Ahhh 2, I think"

"Well, do you know for sure or are you guessing?"

"Your partner shot too, didn't she?"

"Ahhhh, I think so, not sure now actually"

"How many rounds did they fire?"

"Dunno, at least one I recall"

"Why did you shoot the suspect?" (easy gimme question setting up for more difficult ones).

"He stabbed a guy then came at us"

"So, you were concerned you would get stabbed yourself?"

"Yes"

"O.K. We are glad you are not hurt. Oh, how far away were you when you pulled the trigger?"

"Ahhh, I dunno, maybe 6 feet?"

"Preliminary measurements put him at 12 feet, but anyways you saw this guy clearly yeah?"

"Yup. Right in front of me"

"O.K. How old would you say he was?"

"20-25"

"White male?"

"Think so, hard to say as it was dark"

"How tall?"

"6 feet"

"Thin, medium, heavy?"

"Big"

"What clothing was he wearing?"

"Jeans maybe, not sure, can't say for sure"

"What color was his shirt?"

"I'm not sure actually"

"Well, you were obviously looking right at him as you told us you shot him, so you must have seen it no? I'll give you a hint. It was a logo of an NHL sports team. Does that help?"

And soon they realize that they can't remember (at this time) much at all.

And we relax them by saying "It's O.K. The important thing was you took action to protect yourself and your partner from being injured or killed. Your brain filtered out the unimportant parts and didn't cloud decision time with all those other "questions". You were in survival mode. Forensics will determine how many rounds you fired and exactly from what distance. If the event wasn't so life threatening, you could probably remember his description and words that were said but none of that was needed at the time of the shooting. Stress is increased when you are at risk of dying. Your mid-brain takes over from the logical/thinking/processing cortex and you respond with what you instinctively "feel" is the proper course of action to stay alive. It's been going on for eons."

"Even with no basic training in firearms (except just the 4 universal firearms safety rules we gave you), you were able to point and shoot at the person because your life depended on it. No aiming was required. In a real close quarter gunfight both eyes are usually instinctively caused to be open to be able to take in as much light and therefore information about the rapidly unfolding violent encounter. Police can, however, aim pistols/rifles when not so close so as to home in on center mass. On the far end of distance, think sniper from 200 yards out. No pressing threat to themselves so time can be spent physical closing an eye and regulating breathing/HR and then perfectly pressing the trigger."

The floor opens up to good questions and a few nervous giggles. To finish off we remind them all that these were just some of the scenarios that officers are given to prepare them for an event of similar nature. They will become blueprints for the brain and body to follow which will increase their and the public's safety.

We also remind them that "In these sims, NOBODY was ACTUALLY trying to harm you. There was NO possibility of physical injury. It was all fake. Completely staged. But based upon your reactions at the moment, the size of your eyes, your flinches, your confusion about what to do and when, we are happy to say that your experience has exposed you to stress. Continued training in these areas will prepare officers for their day. Hopefully now, you have a greater understanding and empathy for an officer when they become instantly embroiled in a deadly force encounter and make life and death decisions in seconds. 1 1000, 2 1000, 3 1000. Yes, in that amount of time it took to read out those numbers. Thank you so much for participating in the class and good night."

Educating the public and media is challenging, time consuming but important. However, it seems the effect quickly wears off and some media and special interest groups still like to vilify and second guess LE. IIWII (It Is What It Is). Don't get too stressed out about it. Just simply understanding that others don't understand helps you understand that some people just don't understand! Breathe my friends, Breathe.

#42 Cops on Camera

So much has been made lately about officers being filmed. Many agencies have moved to issuing their members with body worn cameras. Since the watershed event on March 3, 1991 (Rodney King), people have been filming police while they interact with the public. The standard police counter tactic for that (if they saw they were being recorded) was to yell "Turn of the camera" or put a hand in front of the lens. We are smarter than that now. Handheld phones pop up like curious or scared ostrich or emu heads at almost every call!

Here is what we know now:

Who gives a flying fuche! We encourage people to film good police doing good work. We have NOTHING to hide. We are PROUD of how we interact with the public and suspects. So don't get your feathers in a fluff if a "herd" (yes that's the name of a group of that genus) shows up to your call!

Here are the top 4 things you should say when being filmed while making an arrest:

1. Do you know this person?

If they answer yes, then ask how do they know them? Friend? Family? Just met them tonight? Then ask question 2.

2. Is this possibly a medical issue?

Which in essence is trying to determine if their behavior is linked to a medical issue (epilepsy, diabetic coma, alcohol or drug overdose etc.) *sometimes sugar related illness can appear to be drunkenness. Check for medical bracelets or insulin paraphernalia or cards in wallets etc. If it's not or they don't know them then number 3.

3. It's fine to film Sir, Ma'am, Bud, but please give us some safe space to work.

Safe space is somewhat subjective but as long as they are back far enough that they don't present a risk to the officers/subject or themselves. Usually, a couple of wing spans away will do.

4. If it's ok with you, can you send us the video or to our sergeant when they arrive? It may help in the event of a charge or complaint.

If they say yes, great. Quite often that will make people leave if they don't want to get involved. Lots of times, they may simply go back to putting their head in the sand.

Controversy sells. Let's not put up any unnecessary "for sale" signs.

As mentioned, I have written over 100 Use of Force Opinions for an array of use of force events. Video has helped in so many of those where the officer made decisions in split seconds to protect themselves or someone else. It doesn't tell the whole story but at least a thousand words (in Arial font size 12, justified).

#43 Let the neighborhood breathe

It is important to let the room breathe before making entry. That same rule applies to *all* of your environments. If you have time (and in most cases we do unless active killer/assaulter violence is heard) take a moment and listen. Noise is a tell. Predator animals will listen intently for prey or other predators. Think cat at night. Footsteps (animal paws, noise underfoot, leaves being stepped on) are a tell! Sounds of car doors, breaking glass, prybars on concrete, wood cracking, people whispering all give audible clues. Cigarette smoke in the air. Cologne that the suspect is wearing, hanging in the air like a bad smell!

Speaking of cats, many years ago, there had been a cat burglar on the prowl in East Vancouver for over 2 months. He was entering homes (similar fact MO, knife jimmying ground floor window) and stealing stuff while the occupants were asleep. The neighbourhood was freaking out (understandably). There had been approximately 24 cases. Forensics identified the suspect as Bud C. (30 years old). His crime time was between 3am-5am weekdays only.

My partner and I asked the Sergeant, if call load permitted, if we could set up in the neighborhood and do a static surveillance. We got the green light and told radio we would be out walking around the war zone. *It was called the war zone, not because it was inherently dangerous, but because most of the streets were respectfully named after WW1 and WW2 campaigns and battles. It was also filled with cul de sacs and wynds that are hard to grid.

We climbed up onto the roof of an elementary school to get a bird's eye view of the major roads in and out. Over about 3 hours nothing of interest was happening. Just when we were about to pull the pin (about 0445hrs) we heard a dog viciously barking off in the distance. As I grew up with German Sheperds and other breeds, I interpreted this one to be pretty pissed! It kept on going, so raccoons or cats were ruled out! We climbed down from the roof and walked several blocks towards the commotion. He was really heating up "Come quick" he kept repeating! As we finally got closer, he stopped. Dang!

As we were reasoning that it was probably nothing, a guy walked out from beside a house with a bag in his hands. We watched as he reached into it. He would look at an item and either put it in his pocket or throw it on the ground. Got it, don't need it. Don't got it, need it. Well, that piqued our interest!

Back then we had these goofy radios that when you turned them on at the start of shift, an audible beep would sound so you could tell it was charged. Thanks loser I.T. non tactical designer! Beep Beep Beep went the radio. The dude (later confirmed as Bud C.) looked over and calmly said "Fuck

You!" Quite the asocial predator. We figured he thought we were just nosy neighbors, so we acquiesced and moved out of his sight and hid behind a bush while he continued his forage.

I quietly got on the shitty radio and asked for cover as we may have a BNE disturbed and possibly the wanted party named Bud C. The dispatcher asked for my location and that's when I realized I had no fucking clue which lane we were in! "Start some cars up to the war zone!"

We were in no position to challenge him as our location was unclear, and he is listed on CPIC as Armed and Dangerous, Psychotic, Anti-police and Extremely Violent.

Bud casually walked into the carport and started up a car and backed it out then drove off. We started chasing the vehicle on foot (under the cover of sidewalk trees) while broadcasting the license plate to get the RO address info. It obviously hadn't been reported as stolen 'cause the owners were still fast asleep!

Bud made it up to a major and indicated a left turn westbound. He punched it and took off at a high rate of speed (maybe saw us). I could hear the responding units and saw the beautiful red and blue in the distance. I flagged a citizen down and amazingly he stopped, and I got in and asked to go west. Never got a chance to thank him formally.

K9 and other units picked up the car (a beautiful 80's

Monte Carlo BTW). The pursuit was on, albeit a short one. Bud crashed into a church (never a good thing) and fled on foot heading back eastbound. YIPEE! I jumped out and clambered up an embankment after slushing through a ditch after a failed 6-foot jump! I met Bud and the others just as the land shark locked on it's prey. Bud tried to stab the dog, dropped the knife and then fought with us. He was charged with 24 BNE's and a wrath of other offences. He was sentenced to federal time.

I thought it was a good idea (at the time) to formally thank the neighbor's dog (with a chewy bone) for alerting us that night/morning. Public Relations thought so too! They contacted their media person and off we went to the next-door neighbor's house. I came up with a couple of cheesy bylines for the article: Dog Catches Cat Burglar! Kudo's to Cado (that was the Husky's name). The neighbors and Cado were happy with the outcome.

About 2 years later I received a phone call from a parole officer who asked if I was the officer that arrested Bud for the Canada-wide warrant and the serial break-ins. I recalled it proudly and said "Oh yes, we were, that was a doozie". He asked if I was the one in the newspaper article and again, I said, "Oh yeah, that's correct". He informed me that Mr. C had that clipping taped to his jail cell wall and was looking at it every day doing pushups and chin ups (I hope nothing else).

Sadly, Mr. C is no longer with us. Now at least, I can rest at night like those in the war zone thanks to Cado.

Takeaway: Let the environment (room, building, parking lot, neighborhood) breathe. Sounds tell you things.

#44 3 Boxes to put your stuff in

Over the many seconds, minutes, hours, days, weeks, months, years and decades of seeing the very best and the very worst of human behavior, you get to wondering? What the Hell is going on? Why do people do such awful things to themselves and others? Why did that person live and that person right next to them in the car die? How in the world did that suicidal/homicidal person come to be in that lane with two steak knives and then not listen to those officers' commands to drop them, then charge at them, which in turn drove them to press the trigger? Why did that kid ride his bike onto the roadway at that particular time the driver was distracted, and the traffic light was malfunctioning. And more importantly, what do I need to do to keep my own shit together so that I can still function to help others and be there for my life and family outside of law enforcement?

Acute stress (immediate and nerve racking) can and does often have an adverse effect on police. Chronic buildup (over time) can also have a negative effect on you. There is currently much ado about PTSD and other mental health issues for first responders.

Here's what I learned from a psychologist. It helped me and maybe it will work for you too. He first said one word. "Breathe". And after I realized that was important (which was written on a beautiful little reminder rock on the table) he gave me some tools. Here's one that helped make some sense out of Life (and Death) or at the very least, reduce the toil of trying to figure it out *all* the time:

Create 3 mental but visual boxes. Label them simply:

1. Everyday Stuff (got it, understand what that was, no need for much brainwork here).
2. Holy Crap Stuff (that's really fucked up, but I understand how/ why it all happened even though it didn't seem fair).
3. Absolutely Bizarre Stuff (totally perplexing. No idea how to even process. Tragic. Painful. Random. Catastrophic. So unfair. Why why why? WTF).

Now when you experience calls or events in your life (on or off the job) you can determine what box it needs to go in. Simply label it and see yourself placing it in its respective box. It's far better than having it float around for days, months, years while trying to make sense of it. If you want to revisit it again, then go ahead and open the box, take it out, and explore it some more. If you get some answers, you can always re-title it and put it in the other box.

If not, put it back in and close the lid. Just having a name for it seems to help identify roughly what it is. It is also important to accept that it may never be solved/explained.

These are *your* private boxes under *your* control. Nobody else has a key except you. You own them. You are in control of them. You let them out on your terms.

Another trick to living well on and off the job is taking up a hobby or pastime. Sounds corny but the reality is it occupies the mind with good things and interests and also connects you to other people of like mind. Musical instruments, models, magic, reading, fishing, engines/motors, travelling, outdoor extreme, hockey, lamp building, yoga, scuba, home reno DYI, basketball, chess, gaming, cooking, writing, martial arts, painting, photography, biking, your community Faith or personal house of worship, swimming, golfing, hunting (some people love it. Personally, the only animal I ever hunted was/is two-legged but to each their own). The list of good things to involve yourself in is limitless.

Quite likely my most valuable (mental reset) time for me was spent coaching the boys through endless summers of Little League Baseball! What a hoot! Scrambling around trying to get them and the equipment bag in the truck, with a java in hand and the half-done batter's lineup after little or no sleep on board due to late shift. Then later in the career, the luxury of getting a day shift job which helped with making most practices and games. Mentoring the kids and letting them be themselves and have fun, exercise, burn off stress, and learn the power of sport was great, but most of all, realizing what it means to them to be a part of a team and in cases making lifelong friends.

It's also time for you to chat about nothing coppish with your coaches. Occasionally once trust is established, you may ask your assistant coach if that dad over there is an asshole. He will likely agree so your off-duty intuition was correct! Other than that, it's time to give to yourself and the community. Give Back. Share. Volunteer. Learn about yourself and others. As with the shifts and demands of law enforcement, special days are missed. Make up what you can when you can.

It's also an opportunity to have a cold one (if you partake) and a wrap up pizza party and give each of the kids a musically inspired DVD (back then) of photo and video memories for them to take pride in and laugh at the mistakes and cherish the small victories and fun times of their growth. The DVD becomes more and more precious as the years reel by.

We won some and lost some. We practiced for game situations and potential plays. We played in the cold and the heat, the rain (until the umps and parents had enough) and the blazing sun. We shared sunflower seeds, and bubble gum, laughed and cried (when it hurt). A league championship was finally won, but the real victories were everyday things like seeing a once shy and terrified child, swing the stick and pound a liner past shortstop! A player stealing home for the first time in her life! A miraculously caught fly to right field by the kid who never really knew what was happening! Which is perfectly appropriate to this chapter. In life we like to think we know what's going on but sometimes in reality we don't have a clue! The seemingly randomness of the World.

So, in the grand Universal scheme of things, something's (actual most things) are out of our control. Fact check: Look up in the sky at night and try to figure out where the infinity stops! So just go out there and work/play hard, have fun, and respect your teammates and the other players (the population) and above all try to be Better Than Yesterday.

The smiles and shrieks of the baseball kids never required being placed in a box. I allow them and other beautiful memories I cherish to float freely around with me every day of my life. They are the security blanket that reminds me/us that everybody *isn't* an asshole, and good is more prevalent than bad in the entire scheme of things. The fact that we deal in bad, can tend to consume us, so doing those good things reminds us otherwise.

#45 Spot the Difference

I didn't read much as a kid or an adult. Eyes were bad, needed glasses, bored, got headaches and numerous other excuses. I liked exploring outside, under houses, in hedges, at the beach, in the trails but also looking at pictures better!

However, in the morning newspaper, close to the crossword puzzle (again, not a fan) there was my most favorite brain game called Spot The Difference! There would be two pictures that looked exactly the same, except for tiny little details which you could only see when closely comparing the two side by each!

For example, the Dalmatian hound would have an extra spot, the tree would have one less branch, the boat would be bearing a different ensign flag, etc. I loved it. Never knew why, but boy oh boy I felt like a hawk, wide-eyed, heart-a-pumping searching for the prey! Well, that game carried over to policing in a very significant way which is maybe why I loved the job so much.

Every day at work I would be looking for differences in human and or structural comparisons. Structurally meant, seeing a pattern of a building or vehicle that stood out from the others: Broken/missing window (cars and buildings); door slightly ajar (cars and buildings); toys in yard (with no children around for a longish period of time) to name a few.

Spotting the difference can also be called "hunting for anomalies". The Department of Defense trains operators to recognize such things as High Value Individuals (HVI's) by way of group dynamics and proxemics (greetings, formalities, handshakes, hugs) as well as hierarchy status by relative positions.

At Tel Aviv's International Airport (TLV) observations and threat analysis happens way outside the airport boundaries as staff and security are trained to recognize subversive behavior and body language. Should it require further attention, the targets are tagged, and the next level operators are advised.

"Knowledge (information) is useless if you don't share it," Michio Kaku (1924-present).

Here are some differences that you can spot in urban policing domains that may, and I emphasize may, MAY mean that something may be amiss. Legal rules in every state, province, country, court have articulable cause principles way beyond my scope of knowledge and often are superseded by appellant court rulings. So, know yours well. I would personally, however, like to take a gun off the streets and have the case tossed, as opposed to not doing anything and having that gun kill a cop or other.

"Suspicious" Persons:

When two people are talking, and one or both (but usually one) starts crowing (looking left and right a few times) they are usually looking for police who would be a threat to their pending success for the deal or transaction (drugs/weapons/stolen property). Quite often, the body position of the spine is leaning forward in a hunch, shoulders rolled forward. Primal C-shape in preparation for anticipated stress.

When a buyer of drugs is walking away from a sale, they are usually so engaged with the idea of fixing very soon, that they don't hide the dope in a pocket or other place. They simply close the hand and walk away. Sometimes the pace is quickened and almost looks like an Olympic speed walker gunning for the finish line!

Layers of clothing or long jackets in hotter climates may (again, may) suggest concealment of long guns. Hoodies being raised up while walking towards a shop (albeit very fashionable according to my kids) help conceal identities from witnesses or CCTV at store entrances (recent big city mob rob takeovers).

Next time you go shopping at the grocery store, have a look at the "normal" behavior of the "normal" paying customers. They, like you, will enter the store, maybe stop and visually orient themselves, take a basket or buggy, have an enviro-friendly bag (or not) and begin the somewhat arduous process of finding food for themselves or the family. They proceed in a pattern of right to left (or left to right) and up and down aisles zigzagging (unless only one or two items are needed).

Quite often they will have a paper list in hand or laying in the basket. Sometimes they are reading their list from their phone. Sometimes (a lot) middle-aged males (sometimes mostly) are glancing up at the aisle titles, phone pressed tightly to their ear, taking directions and instructions from HQ about the exact type of panko needed and not to get anything else except for some cat treats, but not the yellow bag, only the orange bag, and while you are there, don't forget the butter sticks, NOT salted and might as well get some bread there instead of at Cobs, but make sure they slice it this time properly, the last one was too thick and…

The thing is, everyone there for a lawful purpose seems to be doing the same thing with a few variations. This behavior is recognized as status quo (Latin: the state in which exists).

Now consider the behavior of a person who is there for nefarious purposes. Immediately, your mind probably went to a product shoplifter (razors, meat, cheese). But let's keep an open mind. My partner and I arrested a sexual predator in the greeting cards aisle of a drug store. While people were searching the shelves for the perfect card (which is an acutely focused task) the suspect was peeking under women's skirts and taking photos. He obviously didn't fit in with the other people at that time and place. He wasn't reading the card he held in hand. It was a prop. The switched-on staff had recognized this anomaly and thankfully called us instead of just scaring him away.

Shoplifters will often be crowing left and right while everyone else is looking up at the aisle title boards. Shoplifters will often have jackets zipped up while others are in lighter clothing (weather dependent). Distraction tactics by others causing commotion or questions to staff requiring attention to be directed away can be used by organized groups.

Belongings (phones, purses) are often left in the "normal" person's shopping carts. A suspect who sees this target will sometimes make a few passes by to see how close he/she can get without causing alarm and also build some familiarity to allow for a closer proxemic without causing fear. They will be stalking the person in the aisles, waiting for them to bend down or reach up or intently read the label and then move in for the crime. Again, think predator behavior. They usually wait for a weak moment before attacking.

Prior to a gun grab, a suspect must see where the officer's holster/pistol is located. This could be a quick but concerted "target glance" at the duty belt. Pre or post that glance, a furtive (sneaky) look, left and right, and maybe over the shoulder for other officers or witnesses, and finally a shift in proxemics to get within actual reaching distance for the gun.

Those three indicators would be classified as a "cluster", and if picked up individually or as a group could lead an officer to simply move off the line, focus on the subject as the priority (instead of on other tasks). If the attack is imminent, then the officer has at least built in a mental preparedness and motor program counter-tactic if it comes to fruition. If the recognition of pre-assault indicators is trained, then a trained response will often follow as the blueprint is already in place.

At a penultimate level, the Boston Bombers (2013) were walking against the crowd at times. Their clothing was different than the other spectators/participants. Most people were smiley faced and yelling words of encouragement for their family or friends nearing the finish line, they were not. One moment they had duffle bags/backpacks, the next moment, they did not. They were out of place for the crowd environmental context and activities.

Prevention is better than extrication.

I was asked by our Major Crime Section to review a file (and associated video) of an attempted murder where the suspect laid in wait before stabbing the victim (drug debt hit).

While the victim stood in line at the local McDonalds, the suspect was pacing back and forth in the block. His right hand was kept in his right jacket pocket for most of the time (approximately 90% of the population is right-handed). He was also wearing a glove on that hand only. Occasionally he would take a knife out of the pocket, open and close it then put it away.

People pace when pensive or nervous. Characteristics of armed subjects (one hand in pocket over time) suggests to us that suspects are making sure the weapon is at the ready and not going to fall out or get fouled up in clothing. Gloves can prevent injury and potential DNA transference, and also provide a grip. Single gloves are a bit of a dead giveaway! Gloves left at scene, another story.

When the victim walked out, the suspect quickly walked up to him and stabbed him in the left side of his neck. The target drops his food bag and stumbles back inside and falls down. Help comes. Victim lives. Suspect arrested not far away. Court defense strategy claimed it was self-defense. Observations and evidence of the subject's behavior leading up to the attack showed pre-meditation and preparedness. Found guilty.

In Patrol one night there was a report of a shooting from a vehicle involved in a road rage several blocks from the police station. I decided to go mobile, have a pinch (not anymore!), and search the district.

About 10 blocks from the scene, I noticed a possible car matching the basic description of the suspect vehicle (white 4 door Acura with out of province plates with several passengers). As I came up to grab the plate, I noticed lots of heads in the car. I dropped back after running it (negative, rental) and waited for units.

The car was driving at normal speeds but the activity in the car was an anomaly. Faces from the back seat were turning and looking back. Lots of bobble head activity. Shoulders dropping, people moving around like a beehive was thrown in there! When my cover cars arrived, we attempted a stop. The pursuit began and lasted about 6 blocks before they blew through a stop sign and collided with a bunch of parked cars.

Containment was set up. We cleared the car. No gun. The dog found one of the suspects and I briefly interviewed him. We had another K9 check the intersection where they made their first turn after we lit them up. He found 5 loaded guns including the Tech 9 that was used in the road rage. After a couple of hours (sun coming up) all the others were located and arrested.

Back story: They were gang members from out of province and were supposed to do a hit on a target but got all caught up (figuratively and literally) in an unrelated road rage!

#46 It's a Numbers Game

The ancient martial arts primary personal weapons ladder is usually numbered 8 for simplicity (that opening sentence wasn't very simple, sorry, getting near the end of the book, hang in there!). Hands 1,2, Elbows 3,4, Knees 5,6, Feet 7,8. In any order basically. Mix and match. Human beings face forward, generally meaning they fight forward so they have 8 basic hitty things. Yes, you can strike with the shoulders in CQB (super cool and actually awesome). We will talk about using your head as a weapon in a wee bit. Now back to the info.

We prepare, and can deal quite well with, One v One.

The problem exists where we have to fight two or more people at once. It is commonly known in police training as "Multiple Assailants". And to clarify, we are not talking about controlling 2 drunks who are lamely falling around or pawing at each other, or 3 college kids who are fighting over some ex-girlfriend/boyfriend, or some shoplifter's friend who is helping push security/police out of the way at the door. We are clearly describing a situation where 2 or more subjects are violently attacking YOU with intent to injure. This will be evident by the fact that they had an opportunity to leave after the initial assault, their dialogue (if speaking) which may include thigs like "Fucking kill this pig piece of shit" "Get his gun" "Fuck you bitch, you're gonna die" etc. and other telltale signs that they are trying to cause serious harm or death.

Heres' the math numbers arithmetic part:

For example, 3 violent suspects equals 8+8+8=24 potential personal weapons they could use to strike you. And because the subjects have the ability to move, those weapons can come from ANY angle (behind/side/under/over etc.). The injury potential extrapolates off the charts when you add in 2 or 3 different angles and available targets. Getting punched in the face seems to be common. Getting forearm smashed in the base of the skull, and kicked in the knee from the side, not so much.

This situation when it occurs is, and should be, considered a Deadly Force Encounter. If somebody tries to tell you, you can finagle your way through this with the least amount of force necessary, and block, shift, shield, parry, deflect, use OC spray, taser, wait for cover etc. please please please send me their contact info. Me and two other instructor buddies will pay our own way to test out THAT strategy.

Court Testimony:

"Yes, your Honor, I can explain that in more detail if it helps to clarify why the officer used techniques that could and did cause grievous bodily harm or death during this event".

"You see, the general public (which includes this jury) believe that because officers are trained and wear protective gear, that they are at some kind of superhero status and have extra fight powers and skill sets to disable even the most villainous of types. The problem is that television, media, and general (but not malicious) ignorance have made that so".

REAL violence is that which we seek to avoid daily. REAL violence is that activity that maims and kills people every day. *On average (according to research by the CDC and DOJ) a person is subjected to violent crime every 40 seconds. A murder occurs, on yearly averages, every 39 minutes. Most people are socially law abiding (thankfully), but some are pure asocial.

REAL violence is what we step in between and face to protect people when they can't protect themselves. REAL violence is REAL. It is dangerous. It looks nothing like a bar fight scene from the highly over-rated Netflix series Yellowstone Season 5 episode 3 or whatever. These are skilled stunt people/actors with sugar-casted "glass" beer bottles (Amazon $45 for 3, buy now receive the 4th one free) and amazingly good sound editors.

The only people who really know what violence is, is those that have been a victim, and those that have been the perpetrator. The rest of us are just hoping it doesn't show up. As it's been said before, "Hope is NOT a strategy".

There used to be a common gang activity posted on various social media sites called "jump ins". Now, the gang members realize that the police can use those videos to identify members and time/location associations and clothing and other evidence etc. so they aren't so common to see. What it looked like was this:

A hopeful prospect of the gang was to arrive at a certain location at a certain time and be "jumped" by the existing members. He/she was not allowed to seriously hurt the "attackers" as that may prove to be injurious and deplete the team. All they were basically supposed to do, was shelter in place (no running away) shield and take a full minute long beating. This would show the others that they were "tough enough" and didn't mind bleeding for each other. It also builds comradery and brother/sisterhood by sharing a highly stressful emotional experience together. Kind of like bonding when we jits roll and experience pain together, and bump knuckles and hug after. Except a lot more fucking brutal and savage. So it's not even close actually for a few reasons. It's not even close to an MMA match either.

Here's the thing: In MMA there are over 25 rules that would result in DQ's or penalizing points. Wait a minute. Back up. Even before the MMA (which BTW I love to watch and dream about a senior's category and fantasize about putting a champion belt over my "flabs" after a round 3 KO by rear naked choke).

Anyways, in an MMA match (or any other sanctioned sporting contest) you know long before the fight where it will occur: In a well-lit building. You also know who your opponent is, and your team can watch his/her/their previous fights before and see their strengths and weaknesses to exploit. You also have a plethora of medical staff watching to ensure your safety if an injury occurs. And the opponent will be within a kilogram of your weight division too! What a dreamy situation. There is a massive disparity between mixed martial arts sport and real fights.

The event also has a time frame down to the second. You get a 10 second beep/bell alert which is always nice to hear if you are getting owned or are winning and just need to make sure you don't get KO'd by a lucky/unlucky one. There is a referee who gets to help you if the risk of injury is seriously imminent. I respect the discipline, dedication, energy and drive, of all sports competitors. But in raging violence against police, or the un-consenting public, it's time to get real.

By the way, in sport fighting you also mostly aren't subjected or have the real concern of being a victim of 25 plus rules which are:

- Butting with the head. *Not a good tactic I believe. Why would you willingly smash your decision maker "computer" into stuff. Take care of your most valuable operating platform (your brain) to protect your hard drive and be able to use your data processor.

- Eye gouging of any kind

- Biting or spitting at an opponent

- Fish hooking (act of inserting a finger or fingers of one or both hands into the mouth or nostrils of a person, pulling away from the centerline of the body)

- Hair pulling

- Spiking an opponent to the canvas on his/her head or neck

- Strikes to the spine or the back of the head

- Throat strikes of any kind, and/or grabbing the trachea

- Fingers outstretched toward an opponent's face/eyes

- Downward pointing elbow strike ('12 to '6 strike)

- Groin attacks of any kind

- Kneeing and/or kicking the head of a grounded opponent

- Stomping a grounded opponent

- Holding opponent's gloves or shorts

- Holding or grabbing the fence or ropes with fingers or toes

- Small joint manipulation

- Throwing opponent out of ring/fighting area

- Intentionally placing a finger into any orifice or any cut or laceration of an opponent

- Clawing, pinching or twisting the flesh

- Timidity (avoiding contact with an opponent, intentionally or consistently dropping the mouthpiece or faking an injury)

- Using abusive language in the fighting area

- Flagrant disregarding of the referee's instructions

- Unsportsmanlike conduct that causes injury to an opponent

- Attacking an opponent after the bell has sounded the end of the period of unarmed combat

- Attacking an opponent on or during the break

- Attacking an opponent who is under the care of the referee

- Interference from a mixed martial artist's corner or seconds

"Well your honor. Let's back up a second and look at that last one. Why is that so dangerous? Because of the angles and ladders mentioned earlier. Plus, the actual context of a police work environment. On the pavement (no mats), with plate glass in store windows (injury potential), with desperate suspects bent on escaping lawful custody, maybe high on drugs/booze or willingly purposefully hurting the officer and the possibility of introducing contact weapons or disarming the officer".

"Thankfully this type of attack doesn't happen often, but when it does and the officer perceives and recognizes a multiple assailant situation and the option of escape or de-escalation dialogue is not present, then the trained tactics must be employed. These should include, but are not limited to, some of the 25 plus rules mixed in with the more valuable practiced skills (Injuring, Shielding, Stacking, Cracking, Re-directing from Modern Warrior™ Legend Phil Messina) which is what the officer did in this incident".

"That is why she/he/they are here today in a capacity to be able to tell the story about their survival and provide evidence to support their decisions and actions which will hopefully convict the suspects of the attempted murder charge. Any further questions?" I didn't think so.

Whoever causes the most injuries, Wins. Whoever quits first, Loses. *See Tim Larkin's Target Focus Training ™ for more details!

#47 The Kids, on Fire

In a lot of my police calls that stood out, (pursuits, gun calls, violent arrests, riots) it always seems I would be in some kind of automatic action. Kind of like a controlled trance. Chasing BNE suspects with buckets of Indigenous art in garbage cans, felt like slow motion. Those were heavy for them which is why they started sacrilegiously dropping heavy jade pieces and keeping the wooden masks! But the whole things seem to unfold precisely, and we would be fully involved without even really thinking (or so we thought). Strange. Auto pilot.

It's always nice knowing that you have functioning kit with you. Radio, Flashlight (2), body armor, duty boots, TK's, firearm, etc. It's a weird, lonely feeling if you don't have it with you. Kind of naked!

On Feb 23rd 2016 at about 0630hrs I was on my way to the VPD Tactical Training Centre where I worked. I was travelling north on Knight Street cresting over the hill at 37th. I noticed a black plume of smoke from a neighborhood about ½ mile away.

As I got closer, the smoke got bigger. Black was not a good sign as most fires when being extinguished get light grey or white. I figured fire services was not on scene yet. It looked very angry and dangerous.

I luckily turned up the proper street, and as I got several houses closer, I could see the flames licking up at the rear of the one on fire. There was a woman outside on the lawn. For some reason I thought it was her house. I called 911 and advised them. Weird not having a radio with instant voices and resources. I parked and ran over.

She said she was a neighbor and believed there were people living inside. We ran up the stairs and banged on the door and began shouting (I recall icy frosty slippery stairs under foot). The door opened and a very sleepy guy asked what was going on. We told him and then he realized what was happening. We asked if there were other people inside and he said "Lots".

The house was being sublet into single room occupancy suites. We went inside and banged on and opened doors, yelling for everyone to get out and dragged them out of bed. Other people were in a dazed and confused state but after some direction they left out the front door. The smoke was getting intense. It had an acrid stench. We all gathered on the front lawn as the home started to hiss, crack, moan and grumble. I asked if there was anyone downstairs and one of the residents said "Yes". We went around the east side of the house but couldn't access much more down the path to the basement rear entrance 'cause it was starting to cook.

There was a ground floor window with white security bars

covering the window. We knocked on the glass and yelled "Wake up! Fire!" hoping the curtains would part. I was thinking how nice it would be to have a baton to smash then rake the glass. Instead, I picked up a ceramic planter and threw it at the window. It, and the glass, broke.

We began furiously yanking the security bars away from the frame. It worked! (Cheap ass materials)! I used the broken flowerpot to rake the glass, then pushing apart the curtains, I climbed inside. It was pitch black. I remember feeling a chest of drawers below the window and lowered myself to the floor. Feeling around, I found a door handle. And then a light switch! Yay, it works still!

I felt for heat on the doorknob (nothing) and then opened the door slowly (remembering a classic movie called Backdraft) and hoping a fire ball didn't erupt with the new oxygen supply. No Ball. I moved into the hallway and there appeared to be another room across just like the one I was in. The curtains seemed to be askew and blowing around. I yelled out. No answer. I moved down the hallway to the back of the house.

There was a ceiling layer of eerie waxy smoke floating around. The rear kitchen area was straight ahead. There were also two rooms to the left. I yelled out. Nada. I made it a little down the hallway where I could hear and see the fire hissing away. It was getting weird. I turned around and made it back to the first room and stood by the broken window and breathed in the fresh good air. Several people had gathered there but none wearing turn out gear, helmets, or Scott Air Packs. Even though the rear of the house was fully involved, it felt quite safe behind the bedroom wall and close to the home-made exit.

All of a sudden, an older guy, who didn't speak much English stuck his head inside and all he said was "Boy! Boy! Boy inside!" For Fucks sake. I missed him. I grabbed a shirt or something from the dresser, stuck it over my mouth. A random guy climbed in through the window and joined me. He was wearing a dark hoody. I started to crawl down the same hallway. It was getting pretty shitty. It was getting murky and felt a lot more dangerous to be in there than a minute before.

I remember I had to take short mouth-to-chest chin tuck type breaths to avoid inhaling deep the crap that tasted really bitter. I made it into both rooms and felt around for some body (anybody) that may have been unconscious there. Nothing. I was on my belly and crawled into the kitchen, the back wall was on fire and all I heard was a tiny little intermittent chirping noise. The lousy smoke alarm with cheap old batteries trying to do their job. What a shit hole. It was eerily quiet. What I saw next was very clear: Both my son's faces staring at me. I remember their expressions were not happy. No Smiling. No "Yay Dad!". They were mad. Mad as Hell. What I read on those faces was "If you die in here, we are really gonna be pissed off, now get the fuck out".

I turned around and crawled back to the safe room. By then numerous heads were perched in the window and yelling for me to get out as the house started to really catch. I climbed out. Then I looked back in, the hooded dude was stuck clambering up the chest of drawers. I grabbed his arm and pulled him out. Just as that happened what I described to investigators was a "rolling black tire of smoke" came chasing us out the window. The place was fully on fire.

On the front lawn were firefighters lining up hoses and setting up to engage to fire. We all moved onto the sidewalk. Ambulances arrived and began assessing the victims. Several cops showed up who looked surprised to see me standing there hacking a lung out and smelling like a smoked trout.

I was terrified that the fire would be put out and a body or pet that I may have missed would be recovered. I told them about the boy inside. They quickly found out that the "boy" was an African student who was renting the room that I saw with the wacky curtains. He wasn't really a boy, he was 20, but the old man knew and described him as a boy! Perspective and communication is everything!

Apparently when I was noisily smashing in and yelling, he

woke up, looked down the hallway to the kitchen and busted out his security barred window and climbed out (hence the curtains all caught up in the glass)! What a morning. Of course, my workmates told me the guy in the hoody was none other than the Grim Reaper and that my biggest mistake was helping him out of the house.

Big takeaway here was listen to your gut and be open to the very primal but also complex nerve center of your most powerful tool. Your Brain. Not only will it help solve problems, but it can also alert you to deep personal and social and emotional values. It's actually really mind blowing! Also, don't wear flip flops to work. I had runners on. It was, after all, in the winter but still if you have to fight or walk over glass or other hazards its best to have protection for the feet!

Years back I had to fight a violent shoplifter on a day off and hold him down for the police after he boosted DVD's from a store. My lame summer loafers fell off and my feet were sore as Hell! Putting on a full uniform is comforting knowing that you have many tools at hand to help solve problems. Off duty "work" feels naked and a little bit vulnerable. I carry a TK in my car in case I come across an officer down or injured citizen. I have a window breaking/seatbelt cutting tool on my key chains. As the saying goes: "Better to have and not need, than need and not have" (Franz Kafka 1883-1924).

48 Perception IS Reality

December 7th 2002 at about 2200hrs I was a patrol sergeant working our downtown eastside. I was sitting in the car by the Science World Expo jamming down a not so healthy Burger King chicken sandwich (with extra lettuce, so kinda healthier). 2 for 1 night!

A squad mate came over the radio saying he just located an unoccupied parked stolen Toyota in the 400 Blk of E. Pender Street and has disabled it. I noticed a guy pushing a shopping cart walk by and I asked him if he was hungry and gave him my dinner through the window (one good deed deserves another). I asked on the air for a dog car. Tied up. I asked for a plainclothes unit. Tied up. It was starting to sound like a supervisor's promotional scenario question! No other units available so I headed over and parked a couple of blocks away.

There is a very active park not far where dope is the trading commodity. The suspect was probably there. We switched over to a Tac Channel to set up on the vehicle. Darren had the eye from across the street.

Moments later Darren said someone was near the car (likely crowing) then walked away, then called "He's inside". All happened pretty fast before any eventual resources were gathered. I drove in from the west and pulled up directly in front of the Camray and activated the takedown lights (night suns). The lone occupant (later ID'd as Thomas S.) was lit up like a Christmas tree. It was very clear to see everything. Darren approached from the driver's side at which time Thomas slapped the door lock down. Darren began smashing at the window with his baton while the suspect unsuccessfully tried to start the car with a screwdriver.

I was standing directly in front of the car (knowing that Darren knows how to make cars inoperable) and figured the window will go soon and then I will move around to Darren's side and pull the guy out and arrest him for Possession of Stolen Property etc. He looked a little suspy and like he had been around the block a few times. Maybe some warrants too was always a possibility.

The next thing the suspect does is produce a crack pipe and a lighter and frantically begins to light it. *Over my years of working in that District, people are literally living hour to hour, day to day and need a hit before they go to jail. Many times when walking up and confirming warrants on people, they would smoke or shoot their last bit of drugs to get them through the jail booking. It was pretty sad, but we wouldn't make a big deal about it and therefore not have to fight over infected glass pipes or needles. Most of the time they would just do it, cap it, and turn around and get cuffed. No biggie. That's what I believed was happening here…Except.

Thomas was leaning away from the pending glass smashing from the baton strikes while still hurriedly trying to connect the flame to the end of the pipe. That is when his jacket moved away from his waistline, and I saw a pistol in his waistband. It was silver with a wooden grip. I immediately called out to Darren "Darren, he's got a gun in the front of his waistband". I don't even remember pulling my gun out but was aware of it in my left hand pointing straight at him. I remember thinking "Holy shit, he doesn't even know we see it but if he does go for it I have a clear shot right from here". We had the jump on him.

At that point Darren dropped his baton and drew his gun. The next thing I recall Thomas doing is looking a little spooked at Darren then at me then he looked down and his right hand moved towards his waist. I shot 3 times as did Darren. I moved to the driver's window beside Darren, and we checked on each other.

I advised radio "2C51 shots fired 400 East Pender, suspect had a gun, officers are ok". The driver's side glass was blown out, Thomas was hunched forward in the seat. The pistol was now on the seat by his groin. I remember thinking if he grabs it again, I will be able to clearly shoot him from the side. He lay motionless. I called out "Don't reach for the gun". Time then sped up a bit as opposed to the slowish motion during the shooting. Sirens, lights and cops then came quickly.

As he was still hunched forward, I took out my flashlight in my non gun hand and lit up his lap. I was puzzled and looked closer. Even closer. I then out loud said "Fuck". Darren asked "What?" I said, "I don't think that's real".

Upon that closer inspection, I was not able to see where the frame, barrel, grip and receiver would separate. It appeared to be a solid mold. Numerous officers arrived and moved us aside and pulled him from the car. As he was taken to the ground, an unmistakable sound of plastic hitting concrete rang out. It was a toy replica. The kind you buy at the dollar store. For fucks sake.

Major Crime discovered that he had been using it for a few weeks to commit robberies (banks) after he escaped from prison back east in Ontario. He had made it out west to Vancouver. The car had been stolen in Burnaby which he was using during the now local crime spree.

At the inquest it was determined that there were three likely explanations for him reaching towards it. I believe he saw we were overtly "upping the response" (from baton and empty-hand to firearm) and looked down realizing it was showing and maybe was trying to conceal it. I didn't think it was a police-precipitated suicide. Maybe, just maybe, he was going to show us that it wasn't real? Either way, our perception was that an armed man, high or getting high, was about to shoot his way out of an arrest for a stolen auto. Perception IS reality.

Side note: One media outlet began running with a story that we had "executed" a guy who was just sitting in a car. No mention of "the gun" or the stolen vehicle in a high crime neighborhood, the drug confused state, or his extensive criminal record including assaults and armed robbery.

Along with other mis-facts that were written in the op-ed articles, I decided to sue the paper and the author for liable/slander etc. because it really fucking pissed me off and blatantly wasn't true. The deceased's brother wanted to support us as well as he mentioned their father held no gripe with what had happened and was sorry Thomas had put us in that position. After meeting with my union, compiling a massive file with evidence and legalese, and inquiring with one of the city's top gun media law firms, the writer was seemingly quietly let go. Funny that. I let it go too. Good Riddance Ms. Joey T. (unscrupulous journalist). Don't fuck with the facts to sell your shitty paper.

#49 "O.K. O.K." and other tricks cop killers play

In Tip # 1 I talked about the day Kenny H. was captured. Several learning points for me and others popped up that fateful morning.

Backstory: My partner Eddie Eviston (who pretty much saved my life) and I were working plainclothes out of our south precinct. That detail usually meant we were reserved for priority calls to be able to get close to a suspect or scene to support patrol officers. We would take calls off the board that wouldn't take too much time to write so that we could stay available city wide if/when needed.

On Christmas eve, we responded to a robbery at the liquor store on Victoria Drive. An employee called 911 after a suspect pistol whipped him and took off with cash and some booze.

We were on scene minutes after the call came in. Suspect GOA. K-9 attended and lost a scent at the rear indicating a car was likely involved. While we were inside waiting for ambulance to attend to the victim, a Robbery Detective (who was working late at the sub-station) called us and said he was enroute to the scene as he had been working on similar MO files. When he arrived, we looked at the surveillance video and he immediately said "That's Kenny H. He should be in prison." He called Canada Corrections and was told KH had walked away from Elbow Lake Penitentiary (formerly a prison about 100km away). High security…NOT.

With that information, a Canada-Wide Warrant was issued for numerous robberies and escape lawful custody. About a week later, a keen-eyed patrol officer spotted an unoccupied parked vehicle in the 300 Block of East 13th Ave. He ran the plate, and it came up as a pointer vehicle associated to Kenny H.

We were mustering for parade in the sub-station when we were called into the Sgt's office. A plan was hatched to set up surveillance on the car and position K9 and other officers in containment in the area and wait for him to return to the car. A target residence was identified from IHL (Incident/premise history records) and it was thought he may be crashing inside.

About an hour into the set, one of the road bosses asked if there was a rear door to the res. Eddie and I walked in between two apartment buildings to get a better look. It was hard to tell. We started walking back out to Sophia Street when a big guy was walking southbound on the near sidewalk. I had never met Kenny H before but the mugshot in my pocket was singing "That's a pretty close match". We didn't draw down on him at that point as we wanted to better assess him and also not draw attention to ourselves so hurriedly without being in a tactically advantageous position.

We were about 20 feet behind him as he approached the intersection. No chance to get on the radio as again, we would have been burned. We only had big patrol radios and no in-ear technology or beans. He stopped at the corner and unnaturally paused, looking left towards the car, and then right towards 13th Ave. He looked over his shoulder at which time Eddie stalled him and said, "Hey Sport, is there a liquor store somewhere around here?" The stall worked 'cause we could see he had nothing in hand and he pointed and said "Yeah, Kingsgate Mall".

At that time, I'm sure he figured we were the cops. Short hair, windbreakers, blue jeans with runners! Eddie then drew his gun and said "Gigs up. Police, get your hands up" I moved over to the sidewalk so we had a triangulation set up (whether that's a good tactic or not it seemed to throw him off). *The situation will often dictate the tactics. Contact weapons, knives, shoulder to shoulder is usually a strong position so that X-fire isn't as big an issue if the suspect runs at one of the officers. Triangulation for gun calls seems to work, as it is harder for suspects to shoot each officer "all at once". He has to turn and find you which provides time for you or your partners to deliver rounds at him (or her) but usually hims. Now back to the shooting...

He replied, "O.K. O.K." and put his right hand above his head but started walking away on the sidewalk towards the car. From the rear I noticed his left arm bent at the elbow with that hand out of my sight but seemed to be moving it around furiously in front of him.

The next thing I see is an outstretched arm towards Eddie with a gun in hand. Eddie started shooting. I thought Kenny was shooting too. I took out my .38 (yes that's how long ago this was) and fired 2 rounds. I thought I was missing as snow was kicking up around and beside him. I fired 2 more. Eddie had fired 11 rounds (SWAT members carried S&W semi autos back then). I fired 4 in total. Kenny then finally fell to the ground.

We moved in. I took the gun out of his hand and threw it in the snow. "Shots fired 13th and Sophia" was broadcast on the radio. Eddie told me to handcuff him. Then time sped up to normal as opposed to the slow-motion experience due to tachypsychia (neurological distortion of time due to stress or trauma).

Backstory: Major Crime Section followed up on the file and found that Kenny had been in the Downtown Eastside the night before at the Patricia Hotel. Autopsy findings discovered 2 times the normal user amount of heroin in his system. Unbeknown to us, he had woken up and had made his way back to the car where we encountered him.

Further investigation found that his pistol (a Luger 9mm

parabellum) had it's safety on. If he had put his left hand up to feign compliance, he would have been able to access the gun with his right hand and then de-activate the safety lever (the Luger was made only for right-handed people). It was the sidearm of choice for the German Waffen SS.

Takeaways:

Always expect the unexpected. We all thought he was in the house near his car.

Wait for the dust/snow to settle. Knowing now what I didn't know then, after the shooting I would have sought cover/concealment behind a tree or car and waited to see if he was still actively hunting for us while lying on the ground. The gun was still in hand, and he could have shot me/us when we moved in (albeit if the safety was off)!

He had shot at a witness who followed him after a bank robbery but was likely not high then, or had readied the gun before the robbery. Forensics found 1 round chambered with 7 in the magazine.

Watch for contradictory messages. Although he said "O.K O.K." he was certainly verbally (and with one hand in the air) faking compliance to gain an advantage. Believe the Body Language over the Words. The two didn't match at all.

Self-criticism: The autopsy report showed 12 injury sites.

Some entrance, some exit, some damaged musculature and limb/arm/hand disfigurements. No .38 rounds were recovered so it showed inconclusive that my rounds fatally wounded him. I was a bit weirdly miffed at this finding. I questioned whether I was any good at performing a life-saving task.

After much later, and speaking with wound analysis, firearms experts, and bio-medical mechanical engineers, it was generally agreed upon that bullets causing minor *or* major injuries cause a flinching reflex and psychological and physical deficits which all add up to dominance and creating windows of opportunity during the chaos. I felt a little better and put it in one of my boxes. Check.

Although Kenny H. didn't do this next trick, some high-risk pre- assault/attack cues are shown by "facial grooming". This is done by way of covering the face with a hand to conceal intent. It is usually a palm towards the face with fingers/palm touching the forehead, eyebrows or nose. It allows the person to glance at potential targets (gun grab) and/or also see when the best time to attack is. The eyes can either look through the splayed fingers or around either side of the hand. Sometimes the mouth is covered to prevent tension/wincing being seen. The index finger can also sit or move back and forth on the upper lip. The head is sometimes tilted down (chin to chest) and the person is able to look through the eyebrows. *These furtive motions do not always mean an attack is imminent. It depends on the totality of circumstances and other essential elements.

A good option is to draw attention to the subject by calling his/her behavior out. "Hey bud, you good?" "You seem a little nervous". Always think "What would I do and when would I do it if I wanted to attack an officer". Calling someone's body language alerts them that you are alert and may deter them from carrying out the attack. Detection and Distance are our friends (yup, that's one of mine…well, the detection added part anyways)!

50 Don't be an asshole

I thought I should just leave this one blank, but it deserves an explanation!

Years ago, I emailed the famous Det. (ret) Lou Savelli NYPD Gang Expert and told him I was presenting to our patrol officers about conducting gang stops and could he share his PowerPoint with me that I saw, and any tips on safely dealing with gang members. He basically said this: Draw a picture of an actual human anatomical sphincter on the whiteboard. Then take a red dry erase marker and draw a circle around it. Then take said red pen and draw a diagonal line through it and simply tell your members, "Don't be assholes!"

I thought back on my many early years in policing. Just like you guys, I dealt with a lot of calls where other cops (I was guilty of a few) had their ego foot swept and had to try to save face with the tough guy BS talk or push people around. That may have worked on some "kids", felt good, and helped the EGO recover and save face BUT...

The vast majority of legit gang members and career criminals have a code: They understand that if they physically resist the cops, they will get taken to the ground and force (justifiable) will be used.

They understand that if they run from the police, K9 or

fast- footed cops will catch them, and if they fight, same earlier rule applies.

They understand that if they draw a weapon on officers, they will be shot. Those are the rules, and they understand and accept them. Fair Game.

However, what they can't accept, at all costs, is if an officer disrespects them or their crew (in any number of ways). "Dis" or "dism" translates to disrespect. Disrespect can translate to Death. Those are the real street gang rules. So, use force only when needed. Be Uber professional and don't be an asshole. Groom the subject for the next officers that deal with him/her/them. It can go a long way towards them not having a massive hate-on for all cops. Keep the lid on the pot type of mentality.

A calm cool composed fit-looking confident cop is way more concerning and unnerving to real crooks than a bully tough guy bravado. Respect garners Respect. A bully cop is one of the greatest officer safety risks after collisions and firearms.

Treating people how you would like to be treated, under similar circumstances, is safer for ALL involved. Take your work seriously, but yourself, not so much! And finally listen to your "gut feelings" also known as intuition. The body and brain have a way of looking after you. Be *alive* to that.

Acknowledgments

This book could not have been written without the knowledge I absorbed from others who I had the honor and pleasure of working with, meeting, and communicating about policing and officer safety tactics over the last 40 plus years. There are many many more than those on the below list. You know who you are.

Thank you so much for the valuable things you all said and did that created an impression, lasted in my memory, and kept me safe and now hopefully will keep others safer. It all comes back to that, at first, physics/chemistry/science saying that "Information is useless unless it is shared". Feel free to share this info to as many people you think could benefit from it.

Be Safe, Train Well. Brother Milli

In alphabetical order (except for Rick).

Sgt. Rick Evans VPD…RIP. My High School Liaison Officer in the 1970's. Our Police Academy Instructor in the 80's. Also, our high school rugby coach too! THE BEST police coach, role model EVER. "I'm watching you mate!" (His daily saying to all of us)!

Sgt. Tom Burns CRT Less Lethal (Excited Delirium pioneer)

D/Chief Ed Eviston (ret) Metro Vancouver Transit Police

Sgt. Joseph "Little Joe" Ferrera Southfield Michigan PD (ret)

Sgt. Al "Goose Man" Gosbee VPD/Class 39 training buddy

Cst. Jim Gravel Delta PD (ret)

Sgt. Don Gulla (ret) Next Level Training™

Cst. Darren "erp" Hall VPD

Sgt. Brad Fawcett VPD (ret)

Cst. Garth Hoffman Delta PD (ret)

S/Sgt. Joel "JJ" Johnston VPD (ret)

Inspector Esko Kajander VPR (ret)

Sgt. Trevor "TK" Kine VPD

Cst. John Irving Esq III VPD

Tim Larkin Target Focused Training™

Inspector John "Bear Fighter" McKay VPD (ret)

Det. Phil Messina NYPD (ret)

Ken Murray, Training at the Speed of Life™

Sgt. Dave "Ogre" Ogilvy Delta PD

Sgt. Jeff Quail Winnipeg Police Service (ret) Setcan Corp.

Sgt. Frank Querido Delta PD (ret)

Sgt. Johnny "BB" Roberts VPD

S/Sgt. Rom Ranallo VPD Firearms Training Team

Dr. George Thompson...RIP

The Vancouver Police Department and the Tactical Training Centre Instructor Cadre that I had the absolute honor and pleasure of working with over the years (we invented LOL)

Sgt. Wayne (The Wu Way) Unger Saanich PD (ret)

Cst. Fiona Weller First FTO VPD (ret)

Brian Willis Winning Mind™

Inspector Coleen Yee VPD

Dave Young USMC (ret) Vistelar Training™

Prof. Marcio Antony 5th degree Blackbelt, Gracie Barra Delta

Every single police recruit that walked through "The Door" and onto the mats that I had the true pleasure of training with and the outstanding group of academy instructors that shared their knowledge about their specialty to "the kids". Thank you Team for your continued support. It all helps. Stay Strong

And finally, my dear Wife, Sons and Family and lifelong friends (and new ones) for their continued support throughout this, and at times, a most difficult, challenging yet rewarding career of public service.

ABOUT THE AUTHOR

Clive was hired by the Vancouver Police Department in 1988. Prior to that he volunteered in the Victim Witness Services Unit providing assistance to victims of crime. He also served 2 years in the Canadian Coast Guard as a rescue seaman and was trained as a ship's diver. His policing career spanned from all patrol districts, mental health and family services Car 86/87 to officer safety training, including a 2-year sentence in Internal Affairs upon being promoted to sergeant (thanks a lot) but his experience in use of force assisted officers who were subject of use of force complaints who were acting in good faith.

He spent 6 years in District 2 (NE) including the Downtown Eastside as a Patrol NCO. He is a court recognized expert in use of force and has taught officer safety tactics in the U.S. and Ireland. He recently taught officer safety to recruits at the provincial police academy which topics included: Ground Fighting; Multiple Assailants; Water Survival; Batons; Team Tactics; Weapon Retention/Retrieval; Edged Weapons Counter Tactics; Tactical Communication and Empty Hand Control. He has written over 100 UOF Opinion Reports for various cases for IA, Civil, Criminal, Coroner's Court and Supreme Court, ranging from simple arm bar takedowns to multiple officer deadly force encounters (Active Shooter).

He holds a black belt (Shodan) in Shotokan Karate (ISKF-JKABC) and also recently began training in Brazilian Jiu Jitsu. He also enjoyed writing his own bio, but for real, it's legit! Be safe fellow swivel heads!

Printed in Great Britain
by Amazon